Interview with an Angel

A novel by
Inelia Benz

Also by Inelia Benz

Interview with an Alien
Interview with a Psychic Assassin

Published by Ascension Media LLC. 2016

© 2016 Inelia Benz. All rights reserved.

No part of this book may be reproduced or transmitted in any form or any manner, electronic or mechanical, including photocopying, recording or by any information storage and retrieval system, without written permission from the author.

Author contact details:
www.inelia.com

Cover by and other graphic art: Maureen Smiley

ISBN: 978-1-365-55399-8

Disclaimer: this book is a novel.

Novels by Inelia Benz

The 13th Mage
Interview with an Alien
Interview with a Psychic Assassin
Interview with an Angel

Other books by Inelia Benz

Are you a Witch?
Personal and Global Ascension 2012-2017
Weekly Empowerment Workbook
The Essential Guide to Spiritual Events

Table of Contents

Chapter One 1
   Introduction 1
   First Interview 3
Chapter Two 24
   Second Interview 24
Chapter Three 39
   Third Interview 41
Chapter Four 62
   Fourth Interview 63
Chapter Five 74
   Fifth Interview 74
Chapter Six 88
   Sixth Interview 90
Chapter Seven 98
   Seventh Interview 98
Chapter Eight 112
   Eighth Interview 115
Chapter Nine 139
   Interview Nine 140
Postscript 164

Chapter One

Introduction

After the extraordinary success of my first two interviews, "Interview with an Alien" and "Interview with a Psychic Assassin", I received many emails from people around the world claiming to be aliens, alien hybrids, MK Ultra trained soldiers, and other extraordinary beings who wanted to be interviewed by me. Some of their stories were indeed verifiable. This book concerns one particular individual who contacted me to let me know that he was, in fact, an Angel.

I would not have taken any particular notice of this unbelievable claim except that in the email, the man mentioned an incident that had happened to me when I was seven years old, where an angel would to come to my bedside, read me bedside stories and tuck me in. He even mentioned to me the first story he had read to me by name. It was one about a little donkey who was too small to carry his load and how he managed to resolve his dilemma. I had never told anyone about this incident except my grandma at the time, and she passed away a long time ago. As an adult I believed my memories of the angel and his visits to have been just the dreams of a child.

I received a few more emails from him, which I must admit took me several months to respond to due to many personal life changes I was going through at the time. I had moved from California to a beautiful little cottage overlooking the ocean in Washington State, gotten engaged and more. Once things had settled down to a more manageable routine, the alleged angel and I agreed to meet at a local eatery in my new home village of Neah Bay. When I walked in for our first meeting, I found him already sitting at my usual table. I recognized him instantly as the angel who had come to me those nights in 1973 when I was just 7 years old. He stood up and walked towards me smiling. Gingery blond short hair, deep golden green eyes, dark skinned, in his 30s or 40s and fit, like someone who works at heavy manual labor.

I smiled to greet him but my eyes welled with tears instead and no words would out. Emotions now well buried overcame my composure. I looked around embarrassed at my crying in such a public place, but no one was staring. He reached out with his arms, I let him hug me. It was like being hugged by a thousand daddies and mommies who made the world beautiful and all the pain go away.

Even writing these words now, months later, fills me with emotion.

Time seemed to stop at that moment as broken pieces from a lifetime here on this Earth came back together and were soothed and healed. When I was finally able to stop sobbing, he cleaned my tears with a napkin and gently led me to my chair. The restaurant sounds started coming back. Conversations nearby, the cook in the kitchen, orders being taken, seagulls and buoys outside, all slowly entered my awareness again and became real. I looked at the man sitting in front of me, wondering if he was going to suddenly vanish as the other reality set in. But he did not. Instead he smiled and told me he had already ordered for us. I looked down to find my usual order was already at the table, waiting for me.

I took my notes, recorder and a pen out of my purse, looked up and asked him if it was ok to record our conversation, he nodded and smiled. I took a sip of my coffee and pressed "record".

The man in this interview introduced himself as Gabriel. The book is presented as a series of questions and answers and although it is called "Interview with an Angel", it can more accurately be described as a mutual discourse and exploration of our own divinity, existence, and meaning within the Universal Superconscious.

And now the disclaimer:

THIS BOOK IS A NOVEL.

First Interview

Inelia Benz: "Why did you contact me via email? Why didn't you just come to me like you did when I was a child?"

Gabriel: "Email is your normal adult form of communication. If I had appeared in your house, you would have probably given me a Taekwondo kick and I would have ended up at the local hospital."

This made me laugh because I was pretty sure that although I probably would have - defended myself - had he suddenly appeared in my house, chances are he would not have needed to go to the ER.

IB: "Ha! I guess you are right, that's probably what I would have done. Tell me, are you really an angel?"

G: "Yes. I am a messenger and helper to human and other beings, working directly from Divine Source. We are known as 'angels', or some might call me an 'archangel'."

IB: "As in "Archangel Gabriel"?"

He nodded and smiled. Images of multiple movies and stories regarding Archangel Gabriel flashed through my mind… not all good. Somehow I knew these movies were anything but accurate.

IB: "How do you like to be called? Archangel? Angel? Gabriel? Or do you have another title you go by personally?"

G: "Gabriel is perfect."

IB: "OK, cool. You mentioned Divine Source. Is that what some people call God?"

G: "Indeed it is, but it is not an entity or singular being as a lot of people seem to think it is. I would like to describe God more as being you. Every human being. Your divine source, and you as divine source. Inseparably so, actually"

At this point I felt my eyes fill with tears again as I remembered the first time we met. I looked down at my notes, trying to compose myself, yes, talking about God was super important. I had a ton of questions about that. The tears burst out and I looked outside the window and wiped them clean again.

G: "Maybe we should talk about that first huh?"

IB: "What?"

G: "The first time we met."

IB: "Why did you visit me Gabriel? A small child in the middle of nowhere and nowhen. Why did you visit every night, read books, tuck me in. And then… vanish. Like you never existed?"

G: "Do you remember how I came to be there? Do you remember why you called me?"

IB: "Yes. I would go to sleep crying every night because my parents had been taken prisoners and placed in concentration camps for being Socialists. They were being tortured so they wouldn't let me tap into them, or visit them astrally. I felt disconnected and alone. My Grandma, whom I was living with at the time, didn't believe in hugs, kisses or story time. But when I couldn't go to sleep one night, and she saw that I was alone and afraid, she gave me a picture of you. She told me you were Gabriel and that it was your job to take care, love and protect all children. That if at any time I felt alone or afraid, I should call you and you would come and stay with me. She then pinned your picture on the wall above my bed.

When she left the room, I took the picture off the wall and looked at every little detail on it. I followed the energy line, the love and light and when I saw you in the Universe, I told you to come to me because I was alone and afraid. I closed my eyes, felt someone sit on the bed, opened my eyes and there you were."

G: "Yes. The way I remember that first day…"

At this point, I saw Gabriel's eyes well with tears too, he looked out the window for a few seconds, then looked back and smiled.

G: "I seem to have gotten something in my eye."

I think he was as shocked as I was by his reaction at the time. For some reason I didn't think Angels could cry very easily or could be overwhelmed by memories and emotions.

G: "What I am, what I have seen and experienced is beyond any words we might find in human language. I have seen the end and beginning of universes. Realities come and go. Yet we persist. We, my species… yes we are a species… have had many jobs, roles, and experiences. Within your realm, the realm of human experience, the angels and archangels who have had the most contact with humanity are categorized, given jobs or roles by humans that bear no actual resemblance to who we are and what we do in reality. Do I protect and look after children? Yes. The birth of children and their survival has been an area that I have taken on, on this planet and others. Some may consider this to be a negative thing. Some will see it as positive. Some cultures and religions picked up on it and teach it broadly. Others have not… Inelia, the times that someone has actually seen me, and not seen a cultural, religious, or sensory projection of their own personality onto me, are few and rare. Why did I come to you in the middle of nowhere and nowhen when you were seven?"

Gabriel became tearful again. I could tell he was shocked at this. He cleared his throat and continued.

G: "I'm sorry. Although I can and do take the shape of man, I am not usually asked to delve so deeply into my own experience of things."

IB: "I find that sometimes yawning, or breathing in slowly and then out super fast helps to stabilize emotions. Are you not familiar with our emotional body, the human emotional body?"

G: "We... our, emotional body is thousands of times stronger and more powerful than that of humans. So yes, this human emotional body is not easily able to contain what I am feeling at the moment."

IB: "What you are feeling?"

Gabriel took a few moments, breathed deeply, exhaled quickly, and then continued.

G: "Existence is possible in an unlimited array of experiences. Unlimited dimensions. Some of these dimensions coexist. Some are accessible to each other. Some are dependent on others. Some are created by the beings who exist in a different one. We, angels, interact with human experience as guardians, guides, debuggers and tweakers. Due to my own roles, I am often sent to Earth to interact with individuals. Yes, to give them messages, to guide them and set them in the right direction. The direction which their own higher self chose for them. It's almost like a glitch is seen and one of us is sent to fix it, guide it back into alignment with the orchestration of experiences on the planet and the person's own choices."

IB: "So, you came to me because there was a glitch in my experience?"

G: "That's the thing. There wasn't. I wasn't sent to you, nor was there any glitch or problem. Yes, I know you were in great pain at the time, but that pain would not have led you to death or the changing of your chosen reality. I was in one part of the multidimensional experience one moment, and then felt a pull, a tug so strong that the next moment I found myself in your house. I looked around expecting to maybe see the creator of existence itself. Instead, I see a tiny human girl sitting on her bed with her eyes closed tight. I tapped into your timeline and saw it had begun seven Earth years earlier. Literally began then. This was new to me. And so I sat next to you. You opened your eyes, looked into mine, asked me to read you a story and handed me your favorite book like there was nothing extraordinary about what had just happened. I was confused as to what my role was supposed to be or what I was supposed to do. You snuggled into my arms, opened the book and pointed at the first paragraph. I read. You fell asleep, I tucked you into bed and left. Then the same thing happened the next day and for many days after that. Then one day it just stopped. I waited. Then I actively looked for you, but I couldn't find you. Then years went past. Still I waited. I knew it was only a matter of time. Sooner or later, I would see you again."

IB: "I forgot about you, didn't I?"

G: "Yes."

IB: "I'm sorry."

G: "No need to be sorry. Your disappearance from my awareness was meant to happen. Your story here on the planet was not about talking with Angels, but about being yourself."

IB: "I thought you abandoned me. I thought you were the one who disappeared."

When I made that statement, I immediately realized that the thought that he had abandoned me didn't come up for me until I was in my late teens, early twenties. I was going through a very painful patch in my life and wondered why Gabriel hadn't been there to protect me like he was supposed to. Or come in and comforted me like he had done when I was a child. I called him but he didn't come.

IB: "How come you are here now Gabriel? How come you found me now? And how come you didn't come to me when I was going through hell here on Earth as a teen and in my twenties and thirties?"

G: "I don't know. People do call on us all the time when they are having a hard time. And if it's part of the choreography, the plans and decisions that have been taken by those individuals and their co-creators, we answer that call. Sometimes they perceive us, and sometimes they don't. Inelia, I can see your timeline now, and see that things would have been different if I had been able to be by your side when you were a teen, or in your twenties and thirties. But for some reason you were invisible to me. I had a knowing that I would see you again. Not a belief, but a knowing. It wasn't until a few months ago that it happened. That I felt your call, and was able to find you on the planet. You pulled me in again like the first time. I was some-when else, then I was by your side. Although, like I said before, I could not materialize into human form next to you. This time it had to be a meeting that conformed with a human adult reality. So I sent you an email."

IB: "I don't remember calling you... or "pulling you in" as you say."

G: "When you were reading all those experiences to decide who you should interview next, you scanned them, all those beings, and thought about what other extraordinary being you would like to interview. Then, suddenly, I was next to you."

IB: "Yes, I remember. I was looking at all those emails and messages, and thought, the person I want to interview next is an Angel. The Angel who came to me when I was a kid. Gabriel. And I remembered your face, and your love, and your laughter, and the stories you would tell me after the books ran out."

We both laugh out loud at the memory of Gabriel telling me stories of his experiences with creatures large and small, about wars (he seemed to be in a lot of wars), the birth of new realities and the death of abandoned ones.

G: "A moment in "when and where" is like an anchor. Like a portal between dimensions, especially if that "when and where" is shared by beings in different dimensions. When you remembered that moment in time, and scanned for me again from that place of love, you were able to find me, and at the same time I was able to find you."

IB: "When I was a little girl, my grandma told me I should not call you all the time just to play or read books because you had more important work to do on Earth and in Heaven. That you had God's work to do. So I stopped. Then I forgot."

G: "It was all as it should be. Or maybe not. You see, a lot of religions and cultures have shut off direct communication between us and people. That's a very good example of how. That we are way too important, or doing important work, so not to call on us for the "little" things. Or sometimes it's the opposite, and a person will feel ok about calling us to find parking spots, but not when they are having a major crisis in their life. This is taught by cultures and religions to cut the person off from their actual support system. A lot of religions also teach people that the only way a person can access us, or God, is through a third party. Not true. If your Grandmother had not said that to you, then it's likely you would not have forgotten about me. Once you forgot about me, I could not find you."

IB: "How come you couldn't find me Gabriel? I thought you could oversee every human on the planet."

G: "Well, I'm not omnipotent. We are not omnipotent. We are a species, like humans are a species. I think it has something to do with your role here. Like I said, your story was not about talking to angels but simply being yourself and everything is as it should be. Or maybe it would have been much easier for you if I had been there but things got hijacked. It's difficult to say at this point. And even if I did answer your call when you were in trouble later on in your life, chances are that neither of us would have recognized the other anyway."

IB: "You say that from looking at my timeline?"

G: "Yes. It's almost like you were wearing a mask, or armor which didn't let your personal signature out."

IB: "Yes, that's true. I got into trouble at a mystical level by fighting with people and beings that were way more powerful than me as a teen. So, to survive, I put on a massively heavy shield around me. Something that would not allow my "light" to show. It wasn't an armor that would protect me from others, it was an armor that stopped others from seeing me.

So I guess, yes, if I called you while wearing that armor, there's no way my message, or energy line, would have reached you. An unexpected side effect that I only see now that we are talking about this. But I took that off in the year 2000, surely after that you would have seen me?"

G: "One would think so. There are some oddities about you that I cannot explain. Like I said, we are not omnipotent. We are just another expression of existence. The universes are still filled with mystery to us. For example, even now, when I scan your timeline, it does not go beyond your present incarnation. Why is that? You are a human being, your timeline should be eternal. And even if your soul was not human in origin, it should still register in the history of existence as an eternal

Source of experience in other planets or dimensions. Just like every other being in the universes."

IB: "You know Gabriel, now that I really look at it, when I was in that dark place, for all those years, I think I actually only thought of you once if at all. And I didn't actually call you. It just felt to me that you had abandoned me."

I looked at Gabriel wondering if I had perhaps projected way too much authority onto him. That perhaps my experience as a child in need had colored my perception of him to be powerful and limitless in awareness and consciousness, instead of seeing him as he is, a divine eternal singular being who was traveling his own journey of evolution through time and space.

I suddenly felt hungry, took a few fries off the plate and put them in my mouth. They were still hot! I looked at my recorder, only a few seconds had gone by since I pressed record.

IB: "Oh my gosh, are we on a different time measurement? We've been chatting for a while now and it's like time has literally not registered."

G: "Yes. You might find that you will need to slow your recording to be able to hear it properly when you get home. You'll probably need to slow it down quite a lot."

IB: "What about the people around us, what do they see?"

G: "They saw us sit down, then lost interest. Most won't even remember we were here. A bit like when you try to remember something you mean to do, but it disappears from your mind."

IB: "Wow, that's a neat trick. Is that part of your toolkit?"

Gabriel smiled.

G: "Yes, part of an angel's toolkit hehehe. Eat your food, before it gets cold."

I felt the environment coming into my awareness again, almost like I had zoned out and then back in again. I could hear the TV, people, seagulls, and smell the food and coffee.

IB: "That is way too awesome Gabriel. I need to know how you do that."

G: "But first I want to know why it is that you don't exist past your birth. Or into the future past your present incarnation for that matter."

IB: "Oh that. Yes. Well… I don't really know. I can tell you my experience of it and maybe you can figure it out."

G: "I would love to hear that."

IB: "OK, but remember that this is an interview about you. People are reading this book because they want to find out all about you, your species, your experiences, and probably your phone number so they can speed dial you. Most of them have already heard the story of my incarnation here a million times."

G: "Yes, of course."

IB: "OK, so, before I incarnated, I was not an 'I', I was a collective consciousness. I experienced existence as a 'we' where individuals exist but do not experience life, emotions, thoughts and all the other things that beings experience, alone or in separateness. Does that word exist? Separateness?"

G: "Yes, it does. Go ahead?"

IB: "Right. Well. 'We' asked this body if she would allow us to incarnate. She was scheduled to die very soon after birth. The body said no, and resisted, but the 'we' convinced her by pulling on her duty cords. 'It's your duty to do this for humanity and the welfare of the planet' type energy. So the body agreed. When the time of death came, the soul that was incarnated in this body left, and suddenly I was no longer a 'we' but an 'I' in the body… which I did not know how to drive. And the rest you can see yourself."

Gabriel looked into my eyes and held my gaze for what felt like an eternity.

G: "Are the 'we' still present? Do you sometimes stop being the 'I' and become 'we' again?"

At this point I started to feel like I was at the doctor's office and he was looking at my tonsils and asking me to say "aaaaahh".

IB: "Well, not quite. It's more like the 'we' used come in and then I would go out of the body. Then there was a period of integration when the 'we' and the 'I' could co-exist in the body. Then it was that the 'I' and the 'we' were half each other's experience. But the interesting thing is that before 'I' was born 'I' did not exist, 'I' was the 'we'. Then suddenly, from one moment to the next, there 'I' was."

G: "If you think back to the moment before you were singular, can you remember who the 'we' were? Or where they came from?"

IB: "It feels like a stepping stone into existence. Like I did not exist. Then my awareness was everything, and nothing. It was pure eternal potentiality. Then I became all that is and isn't. Then there was I and other, me and environment, which apparently I created. Then there were other beings in that reality, which apparently I was also. I was all things, all beings, all times and no time. Then I became just a group of those beings, separate from environment and from other groups and individuals. That group, the one that my awareness became, came to Earth, found a body, and then my awareness went from 'we' to 'I. If I look, I find myself still existing in various awareness points at different levels of existence in that journey. Almost like I have anchor points that go from the start, the non-existent state, to me here in this body on planet Earth. The awareness points are in different densities and levels of experience. Although I may not have a 'history' through eternity, I am anchored there as long as 'I' exist. And when that existence ends, so too do the anchor points of awareness end."

Gabriel nodded, his eyes frowning in deep thought. Then he looked away, still thinking.

Outside the cafe window, above the hills, a large cloud of birds moved through the air. The cloud moved quickly, shifting shape, speed and direction smoothly and effortlessly. As I observed it, it felt like I was all those single birds and one consciousness at the same time.

G: "Do you see those birds?"

IB: "Yes, it always fills me with wonder when I see a bird cloud like that one. How it moves and changes shape, hundreds, or probably thousands of tiny birds moving together, never crashing into each other."

G: "Some beings exist in collective consciousness. Some in singular consciousness. There are elemental consciousness and soul consciousness too. Those birds are singular, but can step in and out of a larger mind. Their collective mind. There are creatures in the Universes that are only material consciousness. They exist as one mind, one consciousness with trillions of singular particles that are their body. A bit like the cells in your body. Each cell is individual and separate but also unable to live outside of the body unless artificially kept alive.

Humans are very much like that. They belong to this collective consciousness, can move in and out of it. A lot of humans have souls from different planets and dimensions, yet, when they enter the human collective, they are very much a human. When they resist the integration into the human collective, it creates a separation not only from humanity, but also from their original soul collective. It gets very lonely and they often don't survive long. It is almost like, by connecting to whom they came here to be, the human collective, they keep their connection to their original collective and their higher self, their divine consciousness, open and healthy. The problem is that most people think that connecting to the human collective means buying into social, cultural and religious programs, devotions and teachings. Not so. It really is about a connection from the heart. It is difficult to do, but worth it. Most species can only tap in and out of their own collectives. Rarely have I seen a being or species that can jump in and out of collectives and minds at will. Or become them. Yet, the human species is able to do just that. Although we have worked with humanity for… well, as long as there has been a human species, there are many dimensions, mysteries and capacities that the human species possesses that are beyond our comprehension.

When you looked at those birds, you became their collective consciousness as well as jumping in and out of different singular selves in that collective."

I thought back to when he asked if I could see the birds, and sure enough, I had indeed done that.

G: "You didn't imagine what it would be like, or borrow into their collective mind, or hear their experiential communication empathically. You became that collective and those individuals."

IB: "Yes, it felt as though I had feathers, and could feel the air in my wings and bugs in my mouth. They are eating bugs by the way, that's why they are moving like that at the moment. And it felt like I had this huge intelligence, and a kind of song with many chirps, that made sense. How did you know? I hadn't even noticed."

G: "It was interesting. It was like seeing a fold in reality. You were no longer here just in human form, but also as them. It was like a double exposure in photography. You were here and being you, but you were also there and being them."

Gabriel looked back at me and smiled.

IB: "That's interesting but I fail to see how it is related to our conversation."

G: "Well, I don't know either actually. But it feels connected to your experience of having come into existence firstly as a collective and then as a singular being. And it feels to me that this is something each person, human person, is stepping into. The capacity to be singularly them, unique and powerful, and whenever they choose, be part of the larger consciousness which is the human collective. Not only that, but maybe also then part of the planetary collective which includes all species on Earth.

In my species, we move through time, can access every known form of time. But we cannot access everywhere, or all locations. Those are hard for us. We can exist in many different forms of time, as well as different points of time, simultaneously. Yet, we cannot exist in different locations. Because you live in a linear time reality, you might think that time and space are intricately connected, that you cannot have one without the other. But that's not exactly accurate.

As a human person, you have déjà vus, you will perceive the future as well as remember the past. Some of you will even have very strong memories of a future that then comes to pass. In that sense, humans have the capacity to move in and out of linear time, as well as to look way ahead or behind the present moment. When a human enters the astral realms, they are then also no longer restricted by location. They can be in one place one moment and in another place the next moment."

IB: "I still don't see the link."

G: "When you remembered, or told me about your birth and about your recollection of the collective consciousness that you were before you became you, I thought I recognized it. The collective. It was a fleeting moment, or time, but I am pretty sure I have had contact with that collective in the past. It is like a memory that refuses to fully surface, yet feels interesting."

At this point, I took my pen and made a note that whatever Gabriel was trying to figure out, although interesting, was not going to be included in the book. I could not see how this was in any way relevant to his own personal story or reason for being here, with us, on the planet.

G: "I would prefer it if you didn't censor me."

IB: "Are you reading my notes?"

G: "You are thinking very loudly, that's all. Still. I would prefer you not censor what I am saying. I understand that you feel this is not interesting or important, and perhaps to you it is not. But to me, and probably your readers, it is. You will be dead and gone one day, and the chance we have to see, explore and map to whatever you are, and whomever the 'we' are, as well as the skills and ways in which you experience reality, will be gone. Yes, I can perceive that you will cease to exist once your body dies, and yes, I can see that that in particular is not really common to other humans. But it feels to me that everything else about you, is where other people can go or do. The more you explore beyond your personal limitations, or limitations you feel humans have, the more you discover what this amazing species, the human species, can do. We, like humans, learn through mapping to other beings and energies. So, even if this is not important to you, or you feel it is boring or common, please let me explore."

IB: "I don't want to have to change the name of the book to "Interview with Inelia". I already told thousands of people it's called, "Interview with an Angel.""

G: "What is the resistance? Why are you hiding who and what you are when the request you received in 2010 was very clear? "Become public. Be yourself.""

I was more than a bit stunned by Gabriel's words. There was a charge behind them, like a passion or very strong request. But still, it felt like I was being told off or made accountable for some sort of crime. I felt like I was being pushed past my comfort zone, and I don't really like being pushed at all.

IB: "I don't see the relevance Gabriel. I have a rule that if something cannot be replicated, or I can't teach people how to do it, then I don't share it. Who or what I am, can or cannot do, is not really relevant. If I can't teach people how to become the bird, and the bird cloud, then talking about it is a waste of time."

G: "If you don't mind me saying, I think that is somewhat shortsighted and… well, patronizing."

IB: "Excuse me?"

G: "You are limiting what others can pick up by your own shortcomings. If you can't figure it out at a mechanical level, you don't share it. Humans, and we, learn by mapping. That means we can tap into an experience while being told of it, and our own… well, operating system one might say, figures out how to do it. Instructions and methodologies are good, but for most things, those can be bypassed with a simple sharing of a story. That is why in every single human culture there are storytellers. In the olden days, storytellers were highly regarded and valued by societies. In my own society, we meet on a regular basis and share our experiences."

IB: "Well, I don't know about that. What I have seen is that there is no point talking about something that cannot be replicated. If I could explain the method or the way in which something like that is done, then sure, it's interesting and worth exploring."

G: "However, humans learn best not through mechanical means or exercise, but through mapping. And the sharing of our experience is the best map a person, or angel, can have to tap into information and capacities. So don't limit people. Don't think that because you have not seen other human beings doing or having skills that you do, that they can't do or learn those skills simply by observing them on you. Even if they insist they cannot do certain things that you can do, because they are human and they think that you are not, share it anyway. They will learn it. It will enter the human collective, and they will expand. Plus, this is my book right? And my own curiosity and exploration is part of it. Yes, we can sit down and have a list of questions that I can answer, but aren't my own questions and discoveries also valuable? What if we explore together and this leads us to answer the big questions together? What if due to your origin, you are a human being that is unlimited by the programs and implants which others have been subjected to, and by expressing who and what you really are, other individuals can free themselves from those programs and implants? You are 100% human while you are in human form. The conclusion then would be that mapping to someone with less limits, makes a life with less limits real."

I wanted to be upset or angry at him. But it didn't come. In a few hours, he had been able to spot and empower me in how to truly empower others. Stop hiding stuff and give individuals the benefit of the doubt. It had always been about expressing things from a different viewpoint anyway. It wasn't like I had ever said anything that hadn't been said before. Well, maybe a few times I had. But who was I to limit human beings when I knew they were limitless? I had a total facepalm moment.

G: "I am not lecturing you. I am exploring, brainstorming. Trying to figure things out."

IB: "I do understand. But I'm not sure I want to be seen, felt or mapped to to that degree. I am much more comfortable being the Observer. Observing rather than being Observed. Plus, most of the time I don't even see the differences between, well anything. But especially between what I think is normal and what others think is normal."

G: "That in itself is interesting because if you don't realize that something is normal, then the only way to share it is if there's a witness. Tell you what, why don't we see where this path of exploration leads us, and then we can tackle one of the questions from your list and see where that leads us? I want to understand "why" you are now. Maybe we will figure it out, and maybe we won't. But the looking and exploring will allow others to map into an experience of being which is probably different to what they have had until now. As you know, humans are unlimited and are creators so, let's move the limitations we have placed on them during this conversation out of the way, and let's see what comes up instead? What do you say?"

IB: "OK, fine. I've always suspected that humans are the original architects of physical experience, and that even those who are here from different planets and dimensions are in fact the original architects who wandered off to other planets for a while. Or maybe they created the entire thing, all the dimensions, physical realities of different densities, different dimensions and the like. It feels like humans created all of physicality."

G: "I remember a time when some species became jealous of humans. I think in part it was because humans expand and grow through witnessing. And this growth does not end with just the human species itself, but expands to every single species that become related to them through DNA or incarnation."

IB: "When you say that other species became jealous of humans, do you mean the myths and religions that talk about Gods becoming jealous? Or Angels becoming jealous? There's even a new mythology talking about the Anunnaki becoming jealous of humans. That was real?"

G: "In a way, yes. Many cultures talk about a war in heaven which was directly related to different factions of a certain species fighting over whether to allow humans to continue to exist."

IB: "You told me about wars in heaven when I was a kid."

G: "Yes. The whole war thing was strange. There were several species that had a huge interest on Earth. They were highly limited themselves, but were very skilled at matter manipulation and the manipulation of DNA. Because Earth was left open, as in genetically modifiable, these species descended onto the Earth to both collect samples and material, and create new creatures that might serve their goals and aspirations."

IB: "Would that be the Anunnaki?"

G: "One of those species was the Anunnaki, yes. There were others too. What was interesting was that when they mixed their own DNA with that of humans, their own species started to transform and change. It was almost like by mixing their DNA with that of humans, a two way ultra-dimensional door was opened. Some of the members of the species were fascinated and pleased about this. But others, the puritans, could not believe this was happening and were not able to know why they could not do that themselves. They first became jealous and tried to isolate the DNA sequence that made that happen, so they could own it. When they could not find it, they became horrified and tried to stop it. But it could not be stopped. They then thought that if they killed all humans, it would go away. The war had two sides, which were made of different species. One side defending the Earth and humans within it, and the other trying to kill everything here. Of course, we took the defensive side. Although we did not take part in the harvesting, seeding or manipulation of DNA, we have always had the role of guides, support and protectors of humans. The human collective did not agree to being eliminated, we heard that decision and we answered by keeping the war outside of the planet and the dimensions where humans exist."

IB: "A certain religion, and maybe more, will teach that the war in heaven was between angels. That some angels became bad, and that the good angels defended heaven against them."

G: "In times gone by, anything that happened in the sky was thought to be about angels. I can tell you now that we are not a divided species. We are very clear in what we do and how we do it. Fear and oppression, or answering the wrath of some heavenly lord is not in our reality."

IB: "Yes. It's almost like everyone really does know that, but we are taught something else. Like, for example, in every country I have lived in, and that's a lot of countries, when someone says, 'oh, look at that child, he's like an angel', or 'you are such an angel', they mean the epitome of goodness and innocence. They don't mean a person or child who is about to commit genocide on an entire population or city."

G: "That's actually quite funny."

I was going to ask another question. But thought perhaps we should call it a day because even though only a few minutes had passed in our human timeline, my reality was that I had been sitting there discussing these very emotionally charged topics for several hours.

IB: "Gabriel? I'm emotionally exhausted right now. What do you say we pick up on our conversation tomorrow?"

G: "Yes, of course. Same time?"

IB: "Yes, this time is perfect. I mean same time tomorrow, not this time over again."

Gabriel laughed.

As I drove to the cabin Larry and I were staying at, it felt like tomorrow could not come fast enough. But I was also relieved for the time I would have to review the recording and my notes as well as soothe my physical and emotional bodies with a long hot shower and a nap.

Chapter Two

When I got back to the cabin, I sat down and reviewed my notes. I switched on the recording and sure enough, I had to upload it onto my computer and slow it down in order to be able to hear the words. It was sped up so much that at first I thought the recording had failed. I couldn't hear anything.

That night I tossed and turned thinking about the day's meeting. Unable to sleep, I got up and went to the kitchen to make a snack. The clock on the stove showed 02:22, I switched on the light and screamed. Yup, there was Gabriel sitting at the kitchen table.

I would have asked him what he was doing there, but I already knew the answer. I had brought him here to continue talking. This was unusual, but felt right. There were so many questions I wanted to ask him, and the previous day's conversation had brought even more to mind.

Second Interview

IB: "Well, welcome to my humble abode. I suppose you've visited the cabin before today, but perhaps without a human body?"

G: "Yes, although I have not come here since your original call a few months back."

IB: "Would you like a cup of tea?"

G: "That would be lovely, thank you."

I put the kettle on and looked out our kitchen window into ocean beyond. The moon was half full and covered the ocean in bright sparkles giving the darkness shape and form. I went to fetch my recorder and notebook. When I returned, one of my kittens, Brad, was sitting on Gabriel's lap, purring away. The clock showed it was 02:24. I put the items on the table and pressed record.

IB: "So we are in regular time speed then?"

G: "Yes, there is no one here that minds our presence."

Gabriel and I smiled, he continued petting the kitten. The kitten certainly didn't mind Gabriel being there, and Larry was fast asleep so he didn't mind either. The kettle hot, I made us some tea and sat in front of him.

IB: "Might as well get on with it I guess. Yesterday at the cafe, you mentioned God. You also mentioned the creator of existence. You said that the first time I pulled you into my reality, you thought you would see the creator of existence. Can you tell me who or what that is?"

G: "Going for the big question right away I see. Well, unlike you, I remember existing always. It is almost as though existence is like an infinity circle, and I was always in it. I don't remember a point where I began, nor do I see a point when I cease to exist. We work as mechanics to universes and creations. Some of those universes and creations, a lot of them, are created by singular or collective minds. A mind or minds will decide to have an experience or reality within matter, for example, and a new matter filled universe is born. The new universe and the collective or singular being become one at many levels. Often then, the universe will become populated by that collective or singular being. And often other collective and singular beings will join them there. But here's the question, who or what created all those singular and collective minds in the first place? Who created the angels, my species, who have always existed? We have been asking this question for as long as I remember. That day in 1973, it felt that only such a being could pull me across dimensions, realities and universes. When I saw you were nothing more than a human girl, and a soul so young that it didn't even register as existing yet, it was clear that there were other forces orchestrating our lives. Something that both of us had agreed to somehow, probably through coinciding goals."

IB: "Geez, you don't pull any punches! 'I thought you were God, but it turned out you are so insignificant that there must be someone else behind all of this.' I'm kidding of course. People will often ask me who or what guides me, or made the request for me to become public, assist certain individuals, or do some energy or mystical work. And the closest I can get is that it is something called the 'Planetary Council', that asks. Basically, what that is, is all of the collective and singular species of this planet who work to manifest a reality of experience which has been decided by all of the species here via consensus. And by the way, that's not their official name, it's just a name I gave them because it was descriptive and conveyed part of their intent and role.

Sometimes it almost feels that I manifested here as a singular person at their request. So maybe it was that Council that made me aware of you by guiding my grandma to give me instructions on how to bring you to me. The force behind it being the ultimate goal of why we are here, which on my end at the moment is to facilitate ways in which people can take their power back and use it themselves. This book will empower people, and will change lives. Just having your consciousness woven into the words and pages of the book will allow people to map to who and what you really are.

There is so much projection and misconception about angels on Earth. Most religions have hijacked what and who you are to further their own power over others game. So yes. This interview will help to dispel a lot of that stuff too.

Going back to topic, if I understand correctly, what you are saying is that even you don't know who your creator is, or the creator of those singular beings and collective consciousnesses that have always existed?"

G: "I have observed how viewpoints of awareness or consciousness are invariably limited to certain dimensional parameters. And that beyond those parameters, the person or being cannot perceive. No matter how big or powerful the being, even the biggest and most powerful, exist within their own… what we might call 'reality'. They have little or no influence, or even capacity to perceive past that reality. So yes. Even though in our reality we, angels, have existed always, that is by itself limited to a reality within time, for example. Time has many expressions, and here on Earth it is mostly experienced as linear. But as you saw yesterday, time can be slowed, stopped, or made faster. It is pliable. Yet, although we have looked, there doesn't seem to be any way to step out of time. We can step outside of linear time, present time and many other expressions of time. But not outside of it entirely. Our conclusion, then, is that whomever created us, must be completely outside time. That's why we cannot see them, it, he or she."

IB: "You know how people on Earth mostly think that they are limited to their own singular self, and a lot of them believe that they are their physical body and cannot think or perceive outside of the physical body's limited perception? Yet you and I both know that most human beings are divine, all powerful beings that exist throughout time and are not limited to their physical environment or body?"

G: "Yes, this is a good example."

IB: "Well, when I ask a person to describe themselves, they will often start by describing their physical body, including their body's sex and age. Sometimes, more often now, they will also describe their goals and passions, desires and dreams. I find that most don't describe themselves as being their own Source of Existence. That they don't describe themselves as The Divine Eternal Consciousness, or God or Goddess that created existence. What they share, indicates the level of reality where they exist in, or are limiting themselves to. And that includes me too! I will often be asked to describe myself. And I find I also limit myself to both my present circumstances, my reality and the reality that I perceive the other person to exist in. So, Gabriel, will you please describe yourself to me?"

Gabriel looked at me and laughed.

G: "Right. Well. I have to think about that."

IB: "Take your time, hehehe."

Gabriel went very quiet for a long time. At first I sat there, waiting, but he looked absent in thought. So I got up and went outside to look at the stars. After a while I too got lost in thoughts. I went back inside when it got too cold for me, to find him still sitting, very still, with a now empty cup in his hands. I put the kettle on again and made him a second cup of tea. I wondered if he had perhaps stopped time for himself so that he could think longer, but for some reason it felt that he was doing this in real time. I took the empty tea cup and put the full one in its place, then sat down. The minutes and then hours went by.

G: "Normally, I think, I believe, I would have answered that question in a very particular way. A lot would have to do with my species, and how we differ to the species of the being who asked that question. And how we are similar also. But the way you set up the question, it made it different. It made my answers feel limited, and more questions came up for me as each answer appeared.

Presently, I would describe myself as curious. Yes. At the moment I am mostly curious as to how this moment came about. I am wondering also about why I describe myself as a being within time. And unable to break out of time. Wondering why I describe my species as always having existed, but not having existed everywhere. We are not everywhere, we are every-when.

We do not have a sex or gender. We do not reproduce. But there again, human souls don't reproduce either. Their bodies do, but their souls don't.

Then I would look as to how we perceive ourselves physically. We are humanoid in appearance but our physical bodies are more subtle and pliable than those of humans. Our body can be no more than light energy one moment, and solid matter the next. The reason being is that our bodies are us, the physical expression of our being and not a different vessel or creature. We resemble the nature of a soul more than a body.

Throughout history human cultures have designated a sex to us. Either male or female. But we do not perceive ourselves as such. We are not dual in nature, either physically or energetically. As we don't reproduce in any way or form, sex, or its equivalent at different vibrational levels, is not a part of our existence. We are individuals, but can connect to our collective at will. We often work in groups, move in groups, explore in groups. But the groups are not static or everlasting. They are very open and fluid.

As individuals, we are very different from each other. Our personality will color the way in which we take on tasks, and how we carry them out, and how we form ourselves physically. In other words, what form we take in the physical, as well as how we are perceived by other species is an aspect of individual expression.

We, each of us, are therefore perceived very differently from each other from within our own species as well as other species. I, for example, have often been identified by humans as being female or mistaken for Jesus in Christian cultures. By other angels, I am seen as physically subtle, smaller than the average angel, warm, soft spoken and patient. Which is why I am regularly requested to take care of situations involving children or warlords.

So… how would I describe myself?

Using your vocabulary, I would say that the first thing that comes to mind would be that we are creations' game-masters. The customer support tech that comes into your computer game and fixes a glitch so you can continue playing. But that's a role. Not who or what we are."

Gabriel became quiet again. After a few minutes he nodded, indicating he was done answering that particular question for now.

IB: "You said you have existed "every-when". That means the future too, our linear future here on Earth, right?"

G: "Yes. All of them."

IB: "In that future… wait, all of them? All our futures? Do you mean Earth's different timelines?"

G: "Yes, and all the timelines of each individual here too. Which are infinite until the person makes them finite, by making them many, then few, then one."

IB: "That's super interesting. Are you saying that a person begins their journey in linear time and they have an infinite number of timelines, but eventually, through choice, their timelines converge into one timeline?"

G: "Yes. This happens at a species level too. The older the species, the less timelines it has."

IB: "Wow… OK. Are you sure about this?"

G: "Well, no, of course I'm not sure about this. It is only my perception of reality. How I see it. How my species sees it. And we are very skilled in time and time-related issues, including timelines. It could very well be that as the person goes through life, more and more timelines fall off our own specific reality perception due to our role in their life, or that species' life. In that scenario, they always have infinite timelines, but we perceive fewer and fewer of them as the being "specializes" in their direction."

IB: "Fascinating. You can see that what your perceived reality is, is not necessarily reality for every other being in the universe. I like that. I was going to ask you if in that future you saw a human species that could easily co-create with your species. Not having you as the nannies as it were, but more of a partnership in creation."

G: "Nannies… hahaha. Hmmm. Well, that indicates something that we haven't discussed. And that is the nature of the human species as creators of reality, while our nature is that of mechanics of reality, or nannies of newly born realities. We don't create reality. And that's partly, I think, why we have been so fascinated by your and other creator species. It's also why we are so willing to participate in any role we can."

IB: "It hadn't occurred to me that maybe some species were not creators of reality. Having lived my entire life with creators all around me, every single human on the planet an unlimited creator, I thought that all species were like that."

G: "As you said, we are limited by our own experience and reality. Sometimes we can assign not just shortcomings to other species, but skills and abilities that they don't actually have onto them. Can I ask you a question?"

IB: "Sure."

G: "How do you perceive me?"

IB: "Ha! That's an interesting question. The answer will obviously illustrate my own limitations and personal reality rather than giving insight into who or what you are.

Well, I am certain that your physical appearance is directly related to the picture I was given of you by my grandmother when I was seven years old. You look exactly like the man in the picture. Except you don't have wings or a halo right now, but I'm pretty sure you did when I was little. Where are your wings by the way?"

G: "The concept of wings originally came from the extrasensory perception of part of our energy body by sensitive people. And the halo is the same.

In the olden days, a few people, those you would nowadays call psychics, drew pictures and depicted us in paintings interpreting the energy they saw behind us as wings. Indeed, we can move it, embrace people with it and it does expand if we float. At a physical level one might say they are like feathered wings."

IB: "You know something super weird?"

G: "What?"

IB: "Since we made the appointment to meet, and I have sensed you in my field of attention, I've felt wings on me. Sometimes I have to sit forward because they get squished if I lean back into the seat. But when I "look" at them, they are gray, not white like yours were. Or golden like those of your friend."

G: "You remember my friend with the golden wings?"

IB: "Yes, of course I remember him. But can you tell me why I grew wings?"

G: "No, I have no idea why you grew wings, and yes I can see them but didn't know you were aware of them. I'm thinking it's the human capacity to map to other species and it won't surprise me at all to find out that there will be readers who will start feeling wings in their body as they read this book too! This is a perfect case of how your subtle bodies are mapping to ours. Gray is the color that they… well let's call them wings, that wings have when they first appear. One might say, they are training wings. As you are new to angels and wings, yours appear grey, but there will be other individuals who have had much contact with us, who will start feeling more mature wings, or had them already. But, now tell me what you remember about my friend with the golden wings."

I should say here that I had actually forgotten about his friend until the moment I asked about the wings and realized that they didn't all come in white like Gabriel's. For me there was no mystery to having forgotten about Gabriel's friend. He was somewhat scary and had only come to visit once when I was a child. It's not like I remembered every single person who ever went to my house or visited with us. Even if they were twenty feet tall, had huge golden wings, red eyes and a flaming sword.

IB: "I remember that he was super tall, that even though we had tall ceilings, he had to crouch down to fit into my bedroom. I remember his scary red eyes, massive golden wings, which were a lot bigger than yours by the way, and I remember his sword. He was also dressed like an ancient roman soldier. Which I know because I've seen plenty of pictures of ancient roman soldiers by now. He also had black hair, looked like he needed a shave, and was whiter than you."

G: "That's about right. Yes. Do you remember his name?"

IB: "No. I don't. But I can sense it was Michael perhaps? I don't know, Michael just popped into my head."

G: "Yes, that was Michael."

Gabriel smiled broadly, looking at me intently. I felt as though I had to share something with him, but wasn't sure what. I looked around half wondering if Michael was standing behind me somewhere. But he wasn't.

IB: "OK, why are you smiling like that?"

G: "Well, because I know of no one who remembers Michael's true projected form. They remember a less scary version of him… sometimes, and mostly people forget they ever saw him. But it makes sense if you also remember what happened when he visited. What do you remember?"

IB: "You arrived and instead of reading a book, you told me a friend of yours wanted to come along, and could he come in. I said "yes", and Michael kind of walked into the room. Only I don't know where he walked in from, because I'm pretty sure the door was too small for him."

G: "Go ahead."

IB: "I remember feeling a little bit afraid, but felt drawn to look into his eyes. They were deep and red or on fire. I could not look away. It felt like he lifted his sword, which was super shiny, or burning, like his eyes. But then all of the sudden, his eyes were fascinating to me. It was like I could see the entire universe through them, and I was no longer afraid. Or my fear was no longer relevant. Then his eyes became as blue and deep as the ocean. I thought about whales and how pretty their song is, and suddenly you were laughing, and he was frowning and looking at me funny. Then I asked him if he wanted to stay and read a book with us but he said it was too uncomfortable in my room because it was too small for him, so he had to go somewhere bigger, with more space. Then it feels like I fell asleep. It feels like we went to the ends of the universe and back again in a dream. It got very confusing."

Gabriel laughed.

G: "Yes. Very well remembered."

IB: "I take it that was Archangel Michael?"

G: "Yes. What happened was… well, firstly let me just state that the being you call Michael is part of the group I work and travel with in this universe. Our group works very closely together and we consider ourselves brothers and sisters. When you pulled me into your life, I discussed the matter thoroughly with my group. Including my brother Michael. Michael, one could say, guards a gate through this particular reality. A gate that goes into a human reality where people can and do exert their creator capacity with less restriction. A reality, also, that doesn't have enslavement or unconsciously played games. No victim and aggressors are possible there."

IB: "And no saviors or martyrs then?"

G: "No saviors or martyrs."

IB: "How refreshing. I have a sense of how he guards that gate or portal. Is it that he will appear to the person as super scary, and if the person runs away, they are not ready for that reality yet?"

G: "Something like that. Fear is just a vibration. An emotional note, like music, it's of a certain pitch that is a core signature of realities based on enslavement, lack and limitations of the beings who are in that reality. Michael has the capacity to tune into that pitch and reflect it back to the person or being to the level that they still have it. If the fear the person feels disables them, then they are basically still enslaved to that energy and moving into a reality where they are fully able to create at all times is not really a good idea. Because most people on Earth would feel fear, and interpret their own reaction to his formidable form as fearful, he has been broadly used to depict a warrior or battling angel. Or defender of groups and religions that are fear based."

IB: "Fear based religions. Yes, that's one of the things I would like to talk to you about too. How your species and individuals in your species are mentioned or described in religions. Do continue though, about the gate Michael guards."

G: "I will try to describe the gate using words you will understand. Of course, it is more than this, but in this particular reality, the human reality, it is basically about going from one chosen reality to another that is being simultaneously played, or inhabited, by the same species. Most souls that are in a power over others universe will be in a linear time frame, and will take millions of what we might call Earth years to reach the end of their power over others reality and be ready and wanting to move on to another reality. When I mentioned to Michael that you had no energy of devotion, worship or fear toward me, he thought he would come in and see if you would react in the same way to him. Plus he was curious and suspicious. Curious of how you fit into the scheme of things during this particular power over others reality. And suspicious about who or what you really were.

I honestly didn't know how you would react, but suspected that you would not fall into fear. And I also requested that he present himself within the reality parameters of a seven year old human child."

IB: "Twenty feet tall, with red eyes, golden wings and a flaming sword? I don't think I had ever seen such a thing. Not even in my brother's history books. I can't really say he appeared within my reality parameters at the time."

G: "No, he cheated somewhat. He suspected you to be pretending to be a seven year old human. And that I was too… naive… to see you for who or what you really were."

IB: "What happened after he left us? All I remember is I fell asleep."

G: "When you stared him down, and I have to qualify that by saying that it was not a competition, at least not for you, he could not figure out how it happened. But, there was nothing hidden in your being. You were wide open and transparent at every level. Although your body reacted with a little fear, it didn't rule you, or affect your spirit of discovery or curiosity. And when you saw whales, well, that disarmed him. He loves whales. They are one of his favorite species on this planet."

"I had to laugh. He left, and that's when things became even more interesting. When he left, you went with him."

IB: "I thought I was invited to travel with him, and it felt like it was a day trip. It's hard to interpret now because I have to see it as I saw it then, as a child, but I also see it as I know life now, as an adult and trained mystic. At the time it felt like he had taken me by the hand and we had gone visiting his home where he had a large room we could sit in and read my book. I am pretty sure I brought my book."

G: "Energetically speaking you are right. He had you in his energy field, his attention field, and curiosity. So when he left, he didn't leave you behind. But most people wouldn't be able to leave their reality like that, so he didn't think to 'drop your hand' as it were. I saw you both vanish, and I went after you. He stopped at a certain point in time and space, and realized he had pulled you along. Of course, this journey was at an astral level and not a physical level for you. Your body was still back in your house, in your bed completely safe in an environment with air and gravity and all the things that a human body needs."

IB: "I don't remember past that point. I remember seeing colors and stars, or what looked like stars. And a feeling that we were floating in space."

G: "When I caught up with you two, you were astrally there, but had gone to sleep. This often happens when a person goes into the astral plane and is not ready for it. Michael was just standing there holding you, not yet sure what to do with you."

IB: "What happened next?"

G: "I had the foresight to leave a time-space marker where your physical body was. We waited for a while to see if you would wake up or would go back to your body yourself, but you didn't do either. This was really not an experience you were ready for, wanted to have, or had chosen to remember. So, we tuned into the marker I had left behind and reached your body. As soon as we got there, your astral form left Michael's arms, reentered your physical body and you stayed asleep."

IB: "What happened with Michael?"

G: "He got teased a lot. But what was interesting was that he couldn't perceive or see you after that. And also, the marker I had left, vanished, so until you pulled me in again, I was not able to find you either. I tried leaving markers after that too, and they all vanished within seconds."

I wanted to ask him why Michael got teased a lot. But I was getting super tired by now. It was close to 5am and I still hadn't gotten any sleep. Gabriel seemed to sense it, and suggested I go to bed for a few hours, and that we could meet again later in the day, when I was rested.

I hugged him goodnight and went back to bed. When I woke up several hours later, he was no longer in the cabin.

Chapter Three

It was after 11am that I got out of bed. I didn't feel particularly well rested, but was very much looking forward to talking to Gabriel again. At the same time, I felt emotionally maxed out. I wondered if I was actually ready to write this book, or if I was even the right person to interview an angel. It felt like my emotional body had been run over by a truck. The thought that I was not strong enough for this was running through my head for the entire morning.

But, I am somewhat stubborn so decided not to give up on it yet.

Knowing that he would come to wherever I was, I decided that our next interview would happen at one of the beaches I love on the Makah Reservation called Tsoo-Yess. The beach is West of the village, and the spot I had in mind is locally known as Strawberry Rock. It is accessed through sacred ground, known as Sacreds to the modern Makah.

After a few hours of reviewing my notes, the recordings, and writing down new questions, I packed a few snacks, bottles of water and left for the beach. It's not open to the public, so I had Larry take me there.

By the time we got there, as predicted by my imagination, the sun was slightly covered by clouds, and the fresh salty air was just the right temperature to hang out for a few hours.

When we got to the rock, we noticed a group of people climbing it, so we walked to the other side and sat on a protruding rock formation which was dry and warm from a morning of sunlight. It didn't take long before I could sense Gabriel. As if on cue, Larry decided he would go and hunt for some prayer rocks. The tide was low and before long he was out of sight. I looked behind and saw Gabriel was walking toward me, flip flops in hand and his trouser legs rolled to mid-calf.

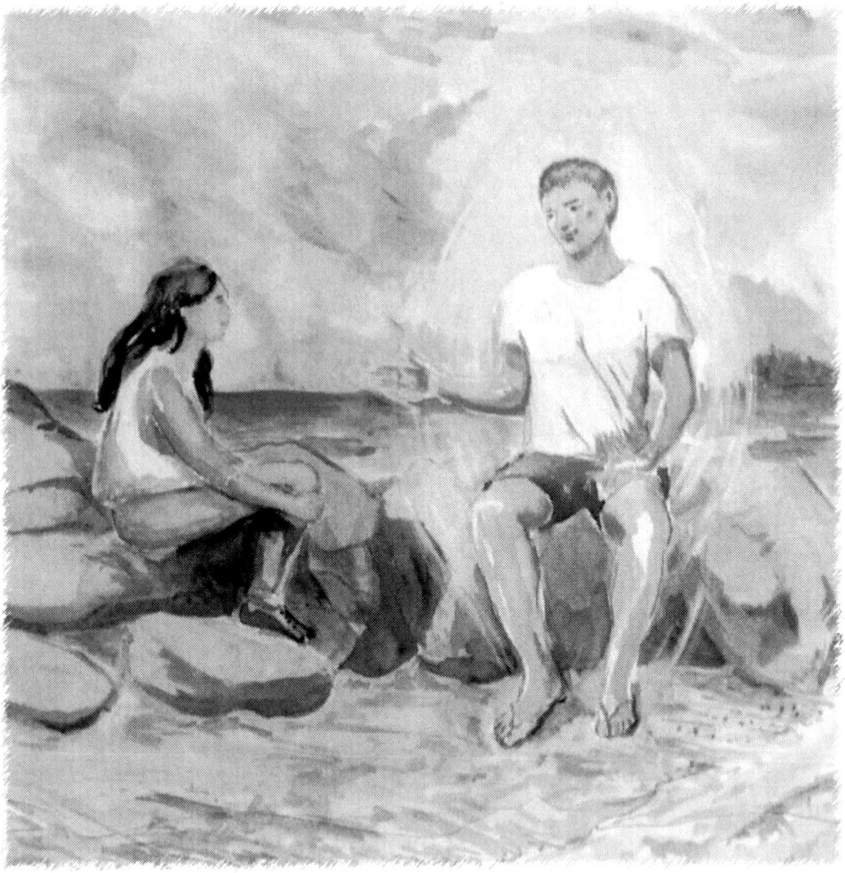

Third Interview

G: "This is such a beautiful spot!"

IB: "Yeah, we come here all the time. Come sit next to me. I brought snacks and water. Actually, now that I think of it, you probably don't need food or water right?"

G: "While embodying a human form, I can need it. In my estimation, the ingestion of food is a form of communication with other humans as well as with the environment."

IB: "Yes, I was coming to the same conclusion about food. Although I don't really get the 'ingesting of other lifeforms to stay alive' part, which seems to be a pretty common theme among Earth species. I would like to talk about it more, but not today."

Gabriel smiled as he sat on the rock next to mine, digging into the snacks. I got comfortable with my notepad and pen, and switched on the recorder.

IB: "I actually have so many questions for you, I don't know which one to ask next!"

G: "I have a few questions too."

IB: "OK, maybe we can take turns. I'll ask a few, then you can ask a few."

G: "Sounds good to me."

IB: "You said last night, well, in the early morning, that Michael got teased after the incident that happened when I was a kid. I find it difficult to imagine that a species as advanced as yours can tease each other about things. Can you expand on what happened?"

G: "Oh, that's a simple one. To use your own words, it appears you are projecting way too much superiority on my species. Or a strange kind of authority, that perhaps because our awareness covers a larger spectrum of reality than yours does, we are somehow without humor and do not make mistakes."

IB: "Yes, I guess you are right on the money on that one. It's difficult for me not to project authority onto you because you are so much more aware of things than I am or anyone else that I have met is. And yes, I suppose I also see the teasing of a person as something that's not particularly positive, so you could not possibly do it to one of your own."

G: "Michael got teased because he unknowingly took you with him. He is extremely able within our own species, so to make such a basic error was highly unusual. For quite a while we would jokingly make him check himself to make sure he didn't have any passengers from distant realities and universes with him. In a way, we all strive for perfection and are very confident in our capacities and abilities. And perhaps teasing is a way to humorously ensure that we stay on the path of attaining perfection. But, at the same time, it was very funny."

Somehow the image of an angel of Michael's size and stature being teased by other angels was actually super funny to me too and I couldn't help laughing out loud. Gabriel nodded and smiled in agreement, knowing he'd gotten the message across.

IB: "Gabriel?"

G: "Yes?"

IB: "Since we've been meeting, I've been feeling things much more strongly. I mean emotions. Sometimes it's almost too much. And the emotions feel very physical too, they burn, or make me feel cold, and other physical things that I don't quite understand. I have to admit that today I toyed with the idea of shelving this book. Not meeting you, and simply forgetting the whole thing. Do you have any idea of why the emotions are so much stronger?"

Gabriel looked at me intently for what seemed to be an eternity.

G: "When you were a child this didn't happen to you?"

IB: "No, it most certainly did not. I don't think I would have even considered interviewing you if that had been the case."

G: "Well, it did happen to me then, and it is happening to me now too. I am finding that the intensity, or volume, of emotions are quite overpowering and difficult to contain. I haven't thought of ending our discussion though. But the emotional wave is certainly something I have to prepare myself for and I brace myself in anticipation of it happening each time. It also doesn't seem to be getting any easier."

IB: "No, it's not getting easier."

We sat there silently for quite a while. Waves of intense emotion would come and go, almost like the waves in the sea. It felt like simply sitting and letting them flow was the right thing to do. The less resistance I felt toward them, the faster and more intense they became. At the same time, I felt my 'wings' stretch out, they were bigger this time, and the feathers were a lighter gray color. I looked over at Gabriel and saw that he was looking at them.

G: "Yes, I see them."

When he said that, I don't know why but I burst into tears. I was crying at something that wasn't mine, but it felt inconsolable. Then I understood. Just like the birds in our first interview, in order to understand and convey what Angels were about, I was becoming one.

I knew it was going to be as temporary as becoming a flock of birds was, but that didn't make it any easier on me or my physical, mental or emotional bodies. Somehow, the becoming of other species on the planet, such as trees, plants, fish, birds, or whatever creature was here, was much easier and didn't have such a dramatic effect on my emotional or mental body as becoming an angel was having. After calming down, I explained my seeing to Gabriel. He nodded and held my hand in his and we were no longer on the planet.

My awareness expanded exponentially, as well as my senses and capacity to feel both my environment and the vibrations we know as emotions. The physical relief of being able to handle the emotions was huge.

We were now in a place that felt like it was contained, almost like an enormous bubble filled with different tastes of energies and colors. I could feel my wings moving, keeping me afloat, my body covered or made of a type of thin film of iridescent colors. I looked beside me and saw Gabriel was there, smiling, still holding my hand and his body was thinner, longer, and neither male nor female. His wings larger than mine, shone white, a golden bubble around his head. Definitely humanoid in shape and form, I understood that it was the closest my human mind would understand and interpret an angel's true form and shape. Around us other angels started appearing from one moment to the next. Soon there were hundreds, then thousands of them. They 'felt' like a symphony. Like sound. Music. I remembered individuals talking about a chorus of angels and now clearly understood why they would be described like that when there were many present at the same time. As I thought that, I also felt a confirmation from Gabriel that yes, other people had come to this place before, and yes, they had described their experience as a chorus of angels. And then, I saw Michael. He appeared just a few feet from us, much larger than most of the other angels and his body seemed to be covered in a metallic looking armor. His wings were bright and golden, his eyes fiery red as though the entire fury of the universe was contained within them.

He smiled.

My wings faltered and I struggled to stay afloat and stable. As I smiled and laughed at this, it felt like my laughter joined the symphony and became contagious. A huge feeling of joy, happiness and humor overcame the entire place.

Michael: "You haven't changed much I see."

IB: "Neither have you! Although now you look more like a science fiction soldier than a roman one."

M: "Ah, yes, the interpretation of your human mind. Can you still feel your human body? Or is it in stasis?"

I felt back to my body, and found it was still sitting on a rock somewhere in the universe, on a planet called Earth, holding Gabriel's human hand.

IB: "I still feel it. It's awake."

M: "Yet you are one of us. And not. You are not eternal and yet you exist always. You have a body like ours and are able to exist in our world. Yet your perception of us is still human and limited. Your timeline is… non-existent past a millisecond ago. Will we know you exist? Or existed once you are no longer here?"

G: "We are still trying to figure all this out Michael."

I could feel a resistance, mainly coming from Michael, but also highly resonant inside of me, to existing in that particular time and space in reality. I held on tighter to Gabriel's hand, and looked into Michael's eyes. The fire inside of them was more intense and consuming than it was during our previous meeting. Almost like this time there was no gentleness to his 'challenge'. I didn't feel fear, competition or aggression. Although I knew that time was at a standstill, it felt like we locked eyes for many days. Suddenly I was him. I was all of them. I could feel their voices, their conversations, their awareness, their journey, their history and their growth. And I saw their origin. A communal gasp was experienced, and suddenly there was solid ground beneath my feet, clear skies around us, and they all became more transparent and fluid. Michael was now about the same size as the other angels. Their voices were like a song. Like a million whispers that create a song one can't quite figure out. It brought to mind the saying 'a chorus of angels' once again. It seemed like I landed on ground beneath my feet, and felt my wings fold on my back. Around us, the landscape became stunningly beautiful. it was exactly like the beach where Gabriel and I were sitting on Earth, but many times more colorful, fluid, and awe inspiring.

IB: "Where are we?"

G: "We are in the same place and space we were before, but your human consciousness is translating it into a form that makes sense to you."

Around us more and more angels appeared, gathering, chatting, and coming over to greet. I felt an enormous amount of curiosity, interest and study projected at me. Their whispers came and went, but I was still unable to figure out what they said.

IB: "It feels like I am not quite as one of you. It feels like the transition is not complete. This is different to when I become one with animals or plants on Earth. There the transition and communication is complete. Here, with you, it feels more like a transient and partial transformation, or joining. Something that 'will do for now' type thing. Plus I can feel that this is a new body, or a transformation of my astral body. When I become one with animals, trees or plants, I become one or many of them at the same time. There is no 'body' that's mine as such. This is certainly different. Here I have my own body. I have wings, and can hear you all, but not understand you."

G: "How do you feel now? Emotionally, energetically and mentally?"

IB: "Super good actually. The emotional exhaustion I was feeling is gone, and I feel a type of freedom. Like a lack of limitations, worries, and a distinct lack of human stuff."

G: "What do you mean by 'human stuff'?"

IB: "I mean importances, relationship links, working in order to pay for basic survival on a planet that belongs to us, having to sleep or eat, addictions and having to relate with people who are clearly asleep and have evil intentions most of the time toward themselves and others."

I stretched my wings out as far as I could, then folded them again. It felt so liberating. So vast and expansive. I heard the whispers, and this time they started to make sense. Mostly they were expressions of friendship and understanding. It felt so cool I did it again, then again!

Spontaneously and without thinking, I let go of Gabriel's hand. Suddenly I felt a flurry of time and space moving through me, like I was in that space, in that bubble, at all times at the same time, and it also was moving through the universe, going through planets and stars. I gasped and reach out with both arms. Several angels held on to me, and made everything settle down. We were back on that amazing, colorful and awe inspiring reproduction of Tsoo-Yess beach.

G: "Whoa, that was a trip!"

IB: "Oh dear, did you feel and see that too?"

Many of the angels said yes, nodded, laughed, and started commenting on the experience.

IB: "What happened?"

G: "Well, like I mentioned before, this 'place' is but a projection of your own human mind that allows you to comprehend and be able to exist and communicate in a time space that is both not linear and really in no particular place. It also appears that your human mind and body had anchored this reality on us holding hands. So when you let go of my hand, it went back to a form that is closer to how we perceive it. But interpreted through your mind. As we are mind joined, we all experienced it."

As Gabriel was talking, I had been looking at the other angels who were still holding my arms. Their touch was so soft and loving, joyful and playful. It made me want to fly, dance, giggle, run, swim, all at the same time. Almost like an agreement, their energies changed, and so did their bodies and mine! We now looked more like little kids with wings, and, still held by two of the angels for stability, we started flying, twirling in the air, diving into the water and out again, and laughing so much it felt the entire universe was laughing with us.

We came back to Gabriel, who was sitting patiently on our rock, filled with happiness, huge smiles on our faces. Gabriel took my hand and the other angels let go. I waved bye to them, and they shifted back to their 'adult' shape and walked away. I looked down and noticed that my iridescent body had also gone back to adult shape and size.

IB: "Wow! That was so much fun! You must love being an angel. It's funny, I love playing, and one of the things I love about people, human people, is that their default is to play too. Put snow on a mountain and thousands will put on rectangular bits of plastic or wood on their feet and swoosh down the mountain just because there is snow there. Or put a body of water anywhere, and they will be playing on the water with their kayaks, paddle-boards, canoes… you name it."

G: "It's true. It is very much part of the human species. It's an amazing energy."

IB: "I've just realized that none of this will be recorded, so I will have to do my best to remember it all. I feel I want to go back now before I forget. Back to the real beach on Earth."

I felt a very powerful sense of urgency, like I knew I would forget all this, or was afraid I would, and before I knew it Gabriel and I were sitting on the rocks at the real Tsoo-Yess beach.

IB: "Well, that was fun."

G: "I know! And I feel much more able to handle the emotions now too."

IB: "Yes, me too."

G: "I'm thinking that some answers won't come by asking questions, but by simply allowing our experience and journey to unfold?"

IB: "Yes, that might be what's happening here. My intention for interviewing you for this book was indeed to get to know you better, and also convey what it is like to be an Angel."

I looked down at my notes. The questions I had written for the day seemed rather infantile and silly after having experienced a full blown ultra dimensional journey into an angel reality. I wondered where that reality was.

IB: "Would you say that the place we went to is a planet? Or is it something different to a planet?"

G: "Not exactly a planet as you understand it. It is more like a compatible, nurturing and supporting environment. It doesn't have a solidity as such, or a shape, or a specific location within the universes. Yes within time though."

IB: "It's so odd. I could have stayed there forever. It felt like I wanted to stay there and explore that energy, location, environment as well as getting to know more angels individually. But for some reason I also, and more urgently, wanted to get back here before I forgot everything that happened there."

G: "It's almost like we are being guided, or given instruction, on how to proceed. I felt the same urge to come back here and do this interview within the limitations of time and space on this planet in a linear fashion. One question at a time, and one after the other."

I grabbed my notepad and pen and wrote some key points down that I knew would remind me of the important bits of the angel's reality and my visit there. After a few minutes I was done, and went back to the questions I had prepared for the day. I was so energized, and so comfortable now, that I could go on for hours.

IB: "This is all so fascinating for me. OK, the next question I have for you on my list is something you already touched upon. You mentioned that you guide people, or come in and fix glitches in people's lives. Many people have reported meeting with angels, or having angels appear to them at critical points in their lives, sometimes saving their lives from car wrecks and such. What I would like to know is why you do this. And how do you know when to turn up. And how come it is not something you do with everyone on the planet, but just a few individuals?"

G: "That's more than one question!"

IB: "Hahaha… yes, it is. OK, so why do you fix glitches in people's lives?"

G: "Why do we fix glitches in people's lives. Well, I already answered that question, but I guess it needs to be explored again, perhaps with different words."

IB: "We did?"

G: "I'm pretty sure we did. Yes. I explained that we are like mechanics, or techs. But I guess that doesn't really explain why we do it. It is like a strong willingness to engage in the co-creation. Maybe if I explain how it feels, what it does in my awareness, in my life, then we can figure out the why we do it.

To me it feels like a homing beacon. Generally speaking, most humans will have a group of beings who travel with them. Don't you call them the person's entourage?"

IB: "Yes I do. It's a group of beings, mostly out of physical body, that guides, teaches, supports, and nourishes the person and their life choices. I have seen several times that some people have angels in their entourage, some people have mostly angels."

G: "Yes, that is accurate. So a person will become like a beacon. Like for some reason, and I don't know the reason, they enter my field of attention. When they are in my field of attention, it is as though I can keep an eye on them at all times. I will often check in on them more thoroughly, but mostly it is running in the background. These will be the people you call 'charges', or the word you used earlier I might be like a nanny to them."

IB: "Oh yes! I too have had people that I am requested to keep in my attention field. I do indeed call them my charges. That's so funny that you would know this."

G: "Well, sometimes I listen in to your public talks, I heard you call the person a 'charge', and the supporting group a person's entourage a few times."

IB: "Ha! That's surprising to me. An Archangel listening to my MP3s and interviews!"

G: "Well, OK so I was snooping around, getting ready for our interview. Like I said, we are not omnipotent, so if you are not one of my charges, I have to find out about you, research and educate myself about you."

IB: "I'm not one of your charges? That's… well, that makes me sad actually. Do I have any angels in my entourage? And why is it not you?"

G: "As far as I can see, there are no angels in your entourage, or there were none. But now I can be, if you let me."

IB: "I have to give you permission?"

G: "Absolutely, that's how it works. No one has a being in their entourage that they didn't give permission to. The request can come from a person, asking for a particular being to be in their entourage, or a being with a particular skill to be there. And the request can come from a being that wants to be part of the guidance and support system of a particular person. When they both agree, and this is mostly done unconsciously by the person and in full consciousness by the being, a match is made. Of course, the joinings are not permanent. They can, and often do, last a lifetime, but most of the time they last only a few years. Sometimes only hours."

IB: "Now that I have spent so much time with you one on one, I can't imagine my life without you by my side. I would love for you to become a permanent member of my entourage."

G: "I'd be honored. And thank you!"

IB: "Do you have a limit on how many people can be your charges?"

G: "Not really. There is no limit to one's awareness, or capacity to hold attention. Except to that dictated by our own set reality limitations of course."

IB: "What about other people who, after reading this book, want you to be part of theirs? Can they call you and request for you to become part of their entourage?"

G: "Yes, that's pretty much how it works. But not everyone will be a perfect match, so the call goes to all of my species, and the most compatible angel, or the one that has the best skills the person needs, will step up to be reviewed and considered."

IB: "And can we request to have more than one angel in our entourage?"

G: "Yes, there are no limits to the size of an entourage or the types of beings that make it up. What I would warn anyone who is actively seeking more members for their entourage is to be aware that there are many beings out there who pretend to have the person's wellbeing in mind, but are actually low vibrational beings hijacking the need or request for support and guidance for their own aggrandizement and agenda."

IB: "How do we make sure that doesn't happen?"

G: "Make sure you state that only high frequency light beings that have your highest happiness and life fulfillment at heart may come near you. And actually, now that we are on the topic, it's always good to purge one's entourage for vibrational compatibility on a regular basis."

IB: "How regularly and how does one do that?"

G: "Once a year at least or whenever you feel you are changing direction in life. And the way to do it, is to call your entourage, so you can do that in an altered state, or in a state of contemplation, and scan them for resonance. Anyone who feels off, or low vibrational you thank for their service, and command to leave."

IB: "I can see that some people might get talked into keeping some low vibrational members of their entourage because they have been with them for a long time, or are relatives they loved."

G: "Well, you can still stay in touch with those beings if you so choose, but you don't really want them to be influential in your life decisions or life path. So, good as occasional visitors if you are into that type of thing, but not as part of your entourage."

IB: "What do you mean by "that type of thing"?"

G: "I mean putting up with, or spending time with low vibrational beings and empowering them in their games."

IB: "Or into thinking one can save them or something like that."

G: "Yes. No one can save someone else from their low vibrational frequency. You can see it very graphically with human addicts. The addict will not stop indulging in the substance they are addicted to until they themselves decide they have had enough and decide to stop. Everything else, the requests for help and asking people to save them, are just routes into getting people to enable their addiction and codependence."

IB: "That's harsh, but I have seen it time and again. That's exactly what they do. Very distracting."

G: "And vampiric. The person has to be honest, when wanting to save an addict, or low vibrational person or entity I would suggest they really question the reason for wanting to save the other person. There is always a low vibrational reason behind it."

IB: "OK, I'll have to think more on that one. I know a lot of people who are easily fooled by low vibrational friends or relatives, and sometimes complete strangers, because they are well meaning and honestly don't think anyone would lie to them like that. How is that low vibrational frequency or motivation?"

G: "It could be one or more of many low vibrational motivations. One is that they themselves want to be perceived as good, kind and think that compassion is expressed best by being soft and taking the painful blows from other people. That's based on the martyr energy, which is low frequency. It could be that they need to save others, but ultimately they are looking to be saved themselves. It could be to appear to others to be a martyr. It could be that they are ignorant of the ways of dark workers, and that's low frequency because ignorance will get you duped and conned, and distracted. Not good results by any standard."

IB: "If we go out of our way to save a person, because the person tells us they cannot save themselves it is often not the right response. Yes, I have seen that used on me before. If the person can't swim, yes, getting in there and pulling them out is humane, but if they run right in and make you jump in again, then it's time to stop and let them learn to swim or drown. I had that happen in real life one time. And you know what? After the person saw I wasn't jumping in for him that time, he swam out of the pool himself. I didn't jump in because I saw he was going to hold me under the water until I died or passed out myself."

G: "That's a good example. Yes, that's what it is like with low vibrational members of an entourage."

IB: "How did they get into the entourage in the first place?"

G: "Well, not every person on the planet is pursuing raising their vibrational frequency. At least they haven't for their entire life. For some years maybe they were indulging in low vibrational life experiences. To have those, the person needs guides that can show them how to have low vibrational experiences. Another way is to think that all ultra-dimensional beings, or every person who has passed away, suddenly becomes high frequency and wants what's best for the individual. Not so. That's why it is important to review and purge an entourage on a regular basis. Sometimes the whole group is in alignment and high vibrational frequency. And sometimes the person might want to go from, for example, becoming an expert surfer, to becoming a computer programmer. Then he or she will need to review and reassemble their entourage to reflect their new passion in life."

IB: "That makes sense. I guess if I see it as them changing interest, rather than vibrational frequency, there is less judgment from me about the purging and choosing of one's entourage.

Going back to what we were discussing earlier, the why you do this. You said you would explain how it felt for you, the mechanics behind it. Can you tell me what happens with your charges? Why you go to them sometimes and don't go to them at other times?"

G: "Yes, of course. I was saying that they are my charges, and that they are always there, in my attention field. Sometimes, as they are in my attention field, one of my charges blips. It looks like a color to me, a point in my attention field that gets brighter. The energy behind the color will tell me what the matter is. It could be an impending emergency, or negative decision, a vibration entering their field that is not compatible with their higher goals, an expansion of awareness…"

IB: "Wait, let me interrupt you there again, did you say a vibration entering their field that is not compatible? Can you explain more about this? What and where would one of these vibrations come from or be?"

G: "Well, it could be a new member of his or her entourage that is way too low frequency for them, or it could be a life experience that they really don't need, or a relationship that is also low frequency."

IB: "What do you do in those cases?"

G: "I would enter their field of attention and point out what is happening. Point out the dissonance, and how it might backfire. How it is derailing them in their chosen path."

IB: "How do you enter their field of attention?"

G: "Some people really do have an open channel to their entourage and will sense us there. In those cases it's like having a conversation in their minds. Often, when this is not the case, we put in a strong feeling, they feel it as an intuition or knowing. At times we also enter their dream state and try to communicate there."

IB: "So when we feel something intuitively, it means you are telling us what to do?"

G: "Sometimes. It's more like we amplify the intuitive knowing of the person. Each person knows when they go into a path that's wrong for them. It's just that often they don't listen to their intuition or inner knowing. We try to make that inner knowing stronger so they can hear it."

IB: "How do you know that the dissonant experience is not something they have chosen?"

G: "We are able to see all their timelines, and some of them don't end well. We try to dissuade them from pursuing that timeline. Basically, if something causes suffering it's really not a good idea to pursue it."

IB: "A lot of people think that everything happens for a reason. That nothing is ultimately negative but is there as a stepping stone to our empowerment or growth. But I have a feeling that you think more like I do, that sometimes the reason for a negative person or situation, is to experience negativity, or to stop, distract or disable us."

G: "Yes, I have witnessed that too. Most negative experiences are there purely for the negative experience. The person can then move out of that negative experience, and most will try to give it value and meaning. But ultimately they would have been much better off in life and in their own power, if they hadn't gone down that path."

IB: "What about children though. Most children who are born to abusive parents or cultures can't just step out of that."

G: "The naïveté of the original decision to be born in hugely negative areas of the world, or families, has large consequences. Most high vibrational beings have no idea, or concept, of what this will mean to their soul or their body. If the child stays in their true essence, and knows that the negative things are happening because other people, dark workers and people indulging in low frequency experience, are doing those things because they want to take the child out, make them an accomplice, or destroy the child not because of something they did, or a decision to "learn from pain" was taken by them, but simply because they came into the planet at a time of war, and is not personal, the child can then overcome what happened to them and not make it into a story or excuse to be cruel themselves, or fall into the false belief that they are a good person because of the tragedy that was their life. They came in being a good person. Having a loving, nurturing and easy environment and experience of life will make them a good and not damaged person. Much more powerful than if they validate or keep the suffering going into adulthood."

IB: "Thank you for confirming that. I have known this since I was a child, and that has been my experience in my personal life. When I dropped the negative experiences and beings from my life, I was then truly able to step into a place of empowerment and be able to more effectively deliver the message of empowerment. And then when I chose to purposely surround myself with mutually supportive, nurturing individuals, everything became amazingly easy and powerful.

When you were describing the reasons for the bleep that you see in your group of charges, you also mentioned an expansion of awareness as being one of those blips that grab your attention. Can you explain what that means and what you do in those cases?"

G: "That's the side of my work which I find to be most exciting. It is when the person, or being, is done with one stage of their experience, and are ready to step into a larger, or different stage. Although of course there are universes which are dedicated to low vibrational games and the movement to lower and lower states of being and narrower awareness states, my species doesn't work with them. We like to work with higher vibrational frequencies and the expansion of awareness. So when someone is ready to step up their game we get notified.

IB: "In those cases, what exactly do you do? I mean, we hear a lot about how angels come to people in their time of need, or during accidents or sickness. But we don't hear very much about angels coming to individuals when they have had an expansion of awareness."

G: "That is true, it seems that the stories people tell are mostly about dramatic incidents. I think that the other side of it, the expansion side, is often not dramatic. Often it is gentle and slow. Sometimes yes, a person can go through a trauma and find that they are a changed person afterward. That they understand life, their mission and their core essence. But that is actually more rare than one might think. But, as it is dramatic, people hear about it more."

IB: "What would be the experience then for a person who you go to because they have decided to expand their awareness?"

G: "From my perspective, I feel that they have a willingness to learn and step out of suffering and pain. In fact, it is often not a passive stepping out of pain and suffering, but active and willful actions in their life that reflect their decision. From their perspective, depending on how aware they are of their entourage, their sense of intuition is strengthened, they are more able to hear their higher self, and some will have active discussions and brainstorming with me."

IB: "I like that you said it is not a passive thing. I am often approached by people who want me to help one of their relatives or friends, save them as it were. Or heal them. And it takes a while for me to get across to them that unless the person themselves wants to learn how to help themselves or heal themselves, there is nothing I can do. I often tell them to send the person who needs help one of my meditations or exercises and advise them to read my webpage articles. But for some strange reason some don't do it. Most do but many people who come in like that don't forward the material to the person in trouble. I'm thinking in these latter cases, the person who asked for another to be saved has an energy of importance, crisis, critical time, savior and… well I sense a lot of times it has to do with the ego. I think that deep down they know that the person in trouble doesn't really want to help themselves but they can rest assured that they at least did the best they could."

G: "Yes, that's very interesting. It is, I think, part of the cultural, social and religious upbringing that says a person cannot help themselves, they need to go to a third party for instruction and passive healing or enlightenment."

I nodded. I wanted to explore what Gabriel thought or knew about religions, but it was getting late. The sun was now very close to the horizon casting a roadway of bright sparkles on the ocean's surface toward us. The tide had also changed and our rock was being stroked by the gentle surf. It would soon be submerged completely. I suddenly felt very tired and at the same time, invigorated, like I had just run a marathon.

IB: "Time to go home I think."

When I said that, my sight seemed to go double, like a double exposure, I could see our reality and also the place where Angels lived. I laughed as I saw one of them wave at me. I waved back. Slowly the other place merged into the sparkles on the water and the birds flying above.

I switched off the recorder, put away my notes and sat quietly for a few minutes as breathed in the fresh sea air.

G: "There is nothing quite like ocean air."

Gabriel took a few deep breaths and smiled broadly.

G: "I guess I'll get going. I see Larry is on his way back."

I looked over to beach in the distance and saw Larry making his way over slowly, looking at the rocks and every now and then, picking something up. I wondered if he had sensed the other reality that had been present a few minutes earlier.

Chapter Four

It was three days later when we met again. After the experience at the beach, all I wanted to do was sleep. It was actually the only thing I could do. Larry would wake me up with food and water every few hours, but I would fall right back to sleep straight afterward.

It's funny when that happens. I always wonder what it's about. As I looked at the energies, it felt very much like the whole emotional body, and physical body had to integrate the past few days into a more resonant vibration.

On the third day, after I woke up and was able enough to get out of bed, I decided to meet Gabriel back at the local restaurant. They were having an Indian fish taco special that I thought Gabriel would enjoy. It was funny, the longer I hang out with him, the more like a regular person he felt to me. As I thought about this, while in the shower, Gabriel simply materialized in front of me. I screamed and told him to get out.

We met for lunch a little while later, and I was right, he loved the fish tacos. It was good to be back at the restaurant. Our first conversation was about our human sense of privacy and how he must not enter the bathroom if I'm having a shower or going to the toilet. In fact, he must never appear in my bathroom again.

Although sunny, it had started raining and we could see waves of raindrops washing over the marina.

I was planning to ask him about one of the major topics around angels: religion. We had touched on the subject a few times in the past few days, but we hadn't really gone into it in depth. After we finished eating, I switched on my recorder but I didn't say anything as I noticed that Gabriel was looking out over the horizon deep in thought.

Fourth Interview

G: "It feels so good here."

IB: "Many people say they feel like they have come home when they get here. I guess it's one of those places on the planet that just feels right."

G: "I can see why. Do you feel that way?"

IB: "Well… I feel peace, warmth and relaxation when crossing into the reservation. Not sure if that qualifies as feeling at home, but it certainly feels a lot better than being outside of here. What I wonder though, why would this land feel so like home to so many people, both Makah and non Makahs, or in my case peaceful, when there is so much hardship here among the residents."

G: "It's probably the disconnect. The Native Nations were fully connected to the land, the planet, the animals and plants. When the last shift came, most all disconnected, which left a big void in their essence. To fill that void is many times harder for a Native Nation person than a Westerner."

IB: "But Western nations also were connected to the land at some point. So, what is the difference between them and a Native Nation person? Why is it felt more strongly in a Native American? Surely the disconnect would have been felt just as strongly in both?"

G: "It has to do with how the separation was reflected in the different cultures. In some cultures, the European ones, it was gradual and it didn't have the energy of displacement as much. There are still families and villages in Europe whose resident families have lived there for thousands of years. Of course there was displacement too, and some races and families were wiped out for all eternity. Also, the villages, then kingdoms and then nations that grew out of the separation, gave people the sense of belonging to something larger than themselves. As it happens, with Native Nations, not only were they displaced, or forced to live in only one place, most of their people were killed and those who were left were forced to forget their native language and culture. So, the link to the land, or identity with a tribe, even now is hard for a person to connect to. There is an energy too, that is present in most people, of 'not belonging'. The energy of separation was such that the disconnect between person and land, environment, and other people is most readily found in a person as a big sense of abandonment, not belonging, and homesickness for a home that never existed. Or a time that never existed. A person will often then create a link to a previous home, or the last soul memory of a home, family, species or tribe. Religion also stepped up big time to fill that particular void."

IB: "Well, I've been studying Native American history, and it's not so pretty or connected. Even here at this tribe, there was a tradition of slavery before the Europeans arrived. And families have been competing with each other for authority and power to this day, conflict and separation is certainly nothing new."

G: "Ah, yes. This is an important thing to remember. The separation didn't come with the Europeans. The shift into the present game of power over others happened at a global level a couple of thousand years before Europe had forts and castles. It is easy to think or believe that all that negativity, separation and exploitation of other human beings began in the Americas, Africa and other colonized continents, after the Europeans arrived. But it is not so. It happened way before and it was the reason why the Europeans were so easily able to conquer just about the entire world. The structures of enslavement were already there, all the Europeans had to do was chop off the head and place their own head there."

IB: "They didn't conquer the entire world though. How about places like China? There were no European settlers there killing Chinese people by the millions. Their race is pretty much unchanged or untouched."

G: "Yet, they dress in western clothes, drive cars, have televisions, live in apartment buildings, built western modeled cities, factories, and lifestyles."

IB: "OK, you got me. I guess they were colonized after all. Not that I know much about China, except what I have seen on television and movies, which is probably not that accurate.

You mentioned that religion had stepped in to fill the void of separation. I want to talk about religions. I know that a lot of readers want to clarify what religions are and why you appear, as a species, in so many of them. The first question then, you mentioned that fear based religions have altered the way in which people perceive you, or connect with you. What I wonder is, how come a religion, or religions in general, are so powerful in overriding your direct connection to your charges. The connection to the people to whom you are supporting as part of their entourage."

G: "We briefly talked about how humans are a creator race, that they create reality from moment to moment. And it's not just solid stuff, but also ideas, entities, and beings. Imagine for a second that a school of thought, a religion, is a living being. A being created from the emotions, beliefs, thoughts, prayers and rituals of people around the world. This being then becomes sentient, and it wants most of all to stay alive. Its survival then becomes more important than anything else, including its followers or their wellbeing. Imagine then, that to survive, this entity, this religion, needs to become needed and necessary in some way. Stepping between Source energy, people's entourages and the people themselves is a perfect way to stay alive and fed."

IB: "Wait a minute. Religions are alive? They are sentient? I don't get it, I thought they were belief systems. Theories, not real and most certainly not alive. You make them sound almost like parasites."

G: "Well, most of them started in a balanced type relationship. They began to balance the disconnect between person, higher self, others and environment. Religion served the believer as much as the believer served the religion. But that's long changed now. Particularly with mainstream large religions on the planet."

IB: "Well, I know individuals who get an enormous sense of peace and support through their religion."

G: "They would not be out of that peaceful state, or in need of support, if their religion didn't encourage a continuous separation from Source in the first place."

IB: "If we invented religions, and they became alive and are now out for their own survival, then why did we invent them in the first place? I mean, every single culture, race or tribe on the planet follows a religion. What's up with that?"

G: "I guess we need to go back to before religions were invented on the planet to understand that one."

I wondered for a moment if we were about to take another field trip, this time through time into the past. Gabriel smiled.

G: "Traveling into the time where there are no religions to take a look is not such a bad idea!"

Everything around me slowed down and stopped. The waitress was pouring fresh coffee into one of the customers cups in front of me, the stream of coffee frozen in midair. Outside the raindrops had stopped where they were. Millions of drops just hanging there! I gasped.

IB: "This is super cool! Wait…"

I wondered about the physical laws of being able to see everything exactly as it was without actual movement through time. Our eyes work from light hitting the retina, and light travels through time, so how were light and images now reaching my retina? I reached out and touched the window. It was solid. I was puzzled

IB: "Wait... "

G: "Physics learned in a linear time fashion will describe everything within linear time perspectives. Do the objects exist outside of linear time? Can light travel? Can our thoughts be formed? Can we move? Yes. Are we moving or is our environment moving and we stand still? Yes."

I laughed. As I laughed I wondered if my laughter was being registered in the minds of the restaurant's customers and staff. I looked outside and examined the raindrops in more detail. They looked like shiny diamonds suspended in the air.

IB: "I want to walk in the rain."

We got up and left the restaurant. Outside, I reached over and touched a drop, it was soft. I grabbed it out of midair to look at it more closely, but as I did that it became just a drop and spread on my fingers and hand. I rubbed my fingers, they were wet.

G: "We are functioning within a limited field of linear time. It is as thin as skin, surrounding our bodies. Once an object or substance enters the field, it also enters linear time."

IB: "Why are we in a field of linear time that's independent of the outside world? I don't understand why it is needed? Why can't we just step outside of it?"

G: "Well, we can. But you would not be able to function very well if we did that. Your physical body, energy field and even the way in which your mind works linearly thought after thought, would all become unusable. It is unlikely you would remember what transpired or that you would even be able to perceive it."

IB: "That makes me feel super limited. Is there any way to step out of those limits?"

G: "Yes."

I felt that his answer was a full stop at the end of a sentence. A stop sign on the road. Or a no entry sign at a gate. There would be no exploration of removing the limitations of linear time existence any time soon. I tapped into the possibility. Around me the world seemed to swerve. I heard a high pitched sound in my head, and suddenly I lost my focus. I was not able to focus on anything or any time.

Gabriel laughed, and I came back to myself, the rain was still suspended in midair, and my thoughts became linear again.

G: "I'll make sure we never go into a room with a big red button that says 'danger, don't press' with you."

I smiled. I knew what he meant, I would probably press it. I know I would press it.

IB: "The time with no religions then."

G: "The time with no religions it is."

I expected a change of scenery, a whoosh sound or something dramatic that would indicate we had travelled through time, but all I saw was us outside the local restaurant one minute and us standing in the woods in front of a campfire the next.

IB: "Where are we?"

G: "When are we... We are before the advent of religion. Or where religion was never invented. It's hard to pinpoint if it's when or where as both exist simultaneously. One might say that this is a timeline where humanity and its environment are still One, or one could say it is your timeline at a point before the separation happened."

IB: "Interesting distinction. Or I should say 'explanation'. I had not thought of timelines as being outside of linear time like that. As in, the equality of our timeline before the separation and a different timeline where separation never happened being one and the same."

G: "Linear time is not really that solid or real. There have been people in history that figured it out to some degree. How fluid and... for lack of a better word how 'unstable' it is. Collective memory is very short. You will find the same social items come up over and over through history, which not many bother to write and even less bother to read. What is also interesting is that when the human collective decides on a certain reality, written proof, memories and solid items appear to support it. So, one could say that this place and time we are on, both existed in your own linear past as well as it existing in a different linear time because it never ceased to exist."

IB: "But what time are we at? In my linear past reality? Or are we in the present time in another timeline?"

Gabriel looked at me puzzled. It was clear I had missed a point, or viewpoint, and he was figuring out how to bridge the idea to me in a way I would understand. Finally, he simply said:

G: "Linear time does not exist."

I actually giggled at his answer. Not so much because what he said was funny, but because the answer was so simple and obvious I found my lack of understanding rather amusing. I looked around.

IB: "I don't see anyone here."

G: "I brought you somewhere that's isolated. There is no one physically near us right now. We came here and now because this is where your people, humans, haven't disconnected from the Earth or their own collective.

Religions began appearing very soon after the separation and only when and where the separation happened. When and where people are no longer able to communicate with each other or the environment telepathically is when adoration to the external began."

IB: "Are you saying that the first religion was a worship of the external environment?"

G: "Yes, that too. Adoration is when the *Word* entered this reality. Adoration means 'to speak or pray'. Speech, prayer, and religion are one and the same. To worship is to speak, or pray to something worthy. Religions sprouted all over the world almost simultaneously. And the objects of worship were external to humans themselves."

It took me a while to digest what Gabriel was saying.

IB: "I have always been fascinated by language, but I had never equated it to religion. I know religion means a strong alignment or allegiance to something. That actually reminds me of a verse in the Christian bible that says, "In the beginning was the Word, and the Word was with God, and the Word was God"."

G: "Words are energy bundles of meaning and vibrations. When the disconnect came, the way to reach others, was through language. The mind also separated from a unified experience interpretation, one might say, of what was happening, to a divided and compartmentalized interpretation of the experience. An alignment is like an energy cord. A line. A connection created and a spoken language used to create that line. Through worship, and words, a person who is disconnected then feels connected to some degree. Not the same degree as they previously felt when there was no separation, but far better than feeling completely disconnected."

I looked around and again thought to myself that there was no one there. Then it came, it was very faint at first, but it got louder. It was not words, but full viewpoints. Almost like being inside several hundred holographic televisions at once and being each and everyone one of the people in those shows at the same time. I closed my eyes and covered my ears, but this only made it louder.

IB: "They are so loud! I don't think I can take this."

The noise of it got super loud, although it wasn't just audible, it was also the visuals. I sensed someone calling my name, I tried to open my eyes and I think I managed to see Gabriel's face. He was saying something, then holding my face toward him and saying it again over and over. I concentrated on his words, and eventually they came through...

G: "Focus on one mile around you. Just think of a one mile radius."

I didn't know what he meant, but he insisted. One mile radius, one mile radius. Eventually the noise, visuals and experiences got smaller and smaller, further and further away leaving but a thin humming behind. And that disappeared too.

G: "You can control the input. Just focus on an area around you, this time we did a mile, but it could be smaller, an inch, a yard, a house, a group of people only or no other people at all. If the group has an identifying signature you can home in and only hear that group."

I became super tired and sleepy, unable to hold my awareness any longer, I fell asleep. When I woke up we were back at the restaurant. It felt like I had nodded off for a few seconds and was now back... food in front of me, the rain hitting the windows next to me, Gabriel smiling in front of me.

IB: "That was intense."

G: "As I walk your world among your people, I hear this noise but created artificially. It's as though your species knows what the natural state really is, and is creating it with radio waves, microwaves and other forms of artificial, low frequency waves. Low frequency compared to your own natural telepathic and empathic broadcasting and receivers. There is so much input around you all the time now."

IB: "Yes, we created the internet too. That's very much a choice input and output within groups or geographical areas. Also artificial. But, and you might be able to confirm this, I have felt that we as a collective species are now more able to tap into the collective mind or database, and to each other. Even people who are fast asleep in their lives, seem to be able to broadcast and receive energy, thoughts and emotions from others more readily."

G: "I would have to agree. Although most of you don't see it, there are radical changes and timeline jumps happening in your world and collective reality all the time."

IB: "Religions then, are creations that came about from the separation of person and environment, and other persons, that somehow became sentient."

G: "Think about it less like its own being, and more like a collective group, vibration, agreement that persists and needs to stay in one piece. Yes, thought forms can become sentient and insist on living on, surviving past their creators and in some cases that is exactly what happened. There are also the cases where a person or being became the object of worship, and that person or being became addicted to the worship."

I was super tired, my mind felt foggy and disconnected. Gabriel noticed and suggested we close it up for the day. I agreed and after eating our meal and talking about dolphins for a while, we called it a day.

Chapter Five

The next day I wondered why religion, and asking him about religions, was so elusive. And why, even though there were far more interesting things to ask him about, the thought of religions did not leave my mind. I wanted to get to the nitty gritty of each of our world's religions, and today that was going to happen come rain or shine!

I was all alone at the cabin, so decided to put in the invitation for Gabriel to meet me there. I put the kettle on and made space on the couch and... put out a chair too. There was someone else coming.

When it was all ready, I heard a knock on the back door, I drew the curtains and there was Gabriel and behind him was Michael. I smiled and let them in.

Michael was wearing clothes, no armor, but true to his energy, they were heavy leather biker clothes, big steel reinforced boots, and he had tattoos on his arms with... Armored angels.

Fifth Interview

IB: "Tattoos? Really?"

M: "What? I think they look cool."

G: "He doesn't spend much time in a regular human body, the tats give him a level of comfort. Like a safety blanket."

Michael frowned at Gabriel's comment. I could tell he didn't know what was being said, but knew it was a joke of some sort. I couldn't help muffling a giggle. I saw what looked like flames flicker in the back of Michael's eyes as he looked at me. It was so easy to forget what these men really were, how powerful and what roles they played in our reality, now that they looked like two regular people.

I had been thinking about Michael a lot since I had met him at the trans-dimensional angel hangout. Gabriel and I hadn't talked much about him, but Michael seemed to be present since then. Almost like a thought that's always there, but doesn't get expressed.

I poured the tea, sat down and switched on my recorders.

IB: "Thank you for coming too Michael. I can't help wondering what made you decide to visit?"

M: "I don't actually know. It felt right."

G: "He's a man of few words."

M: "It feels like I need to be here in this time place with you and Gabriel."

IB: "That's cool. Yes, I have been thinking about you since we last met. Well, not exactly thinking about you. More like feeling your awareness and mind in mine. Hard to explain."

Michael nodded. This was going to be interesting. He really did not speak very much at all but he expressed plenty. Transcribing a body language conversation would be a challenge for sure!

IB: "OK, I will ask some questions, then you both can take turns answering them. How does that sound?"

G: "Sounds good."

Michael frowned.

Yup, it was going to be challenging.

IB: "OK. Religions. I want to pick up on where we left off…"

M: "No."

IB: "No? What do you mean 'no'?"

M: "Religions are too small a topic. We need to talk about something else."

Both Gabriel and I waited for Michael to say more. But he just sat there looking back at us, picked up his cup of tea with his thumb and index finger, pinky up, and went on to daintily sip some tea. I bit my lips so as not to giggle. It was quite a sight, this huge, powerful man in tats and leather biker gear, drinking tea like that. I looked over at Gabriel who was staring at his brother in shock or amazement. Hard to say which.

M: "What."

Gabriel and I both looked away smiling.

IB: "Here's the thing Michael, you are depicted as an archangel in Judaism, Christianity, and Islam. And not only that, but probably the archangel who is closest to God and is always telling people about God and getting them back to the fold. If you don't want to talk about religion that's fine, but can you at least confirm or deny the claims all these religions and religious people make about you?"

M: "Humans think that I work for God. But the thing is that you guys need to reconsider, or redefine what you call God. We are not in the middle ages anymore, you have the capacity and skills to see that there is no external male deity, a father, who made you and the universe. I work for the creator, yes. But the creator is you, all of you. And I most certainly don't bring people into religions. That's a projection and a fantasy probably created from an over-inflated ego. I mean, if an ultra-dimensional being is going to go and get Norma back to Jesus, and Norma is a school girl from Dublin, why would her God send me? Why not send low ranking Tony, the angel of whatever… but no. They always think it's one of the big names. Me, or Gabriel.

IB: "Well, because maybe we have pictures of you and we look at them and call you? I called Gabriel and he came along. Or are you saying you are not really archangels Gabriel and Michael but Tony and Robert from some other dimension who are pretending to be famous archangels? Because it was you guys who told me your names, not me."

M: "There's no need to get cocky. But I get your point. Sometimes the way I express myself sounds like an attack. I do get frustrated when humans choose spoken word to communicate, their slowest and least efficient mode of communication."

IB: "I need to record our conversations, plus I don't exactly know how to write an experiential conversation. Back to what we were talking about though, I understand what religion is. It's a human creation to explain, or keep a link with their higher self, and their collective self after the separation from the environment and their collective consciousness. And the characters in that creation, or fantasy, are given human shape and form by humans so that we can understand it better."

M: "And our role, because we have been diligently working to keep you on your chosen path which for most of you is a strong and deep desire to reconnect to your higher self-awareness, and your collective awareness, has been misinterpreted as us telling you to get back to some old bad tempered, scary guy on a throne who lives in heaven. Or to some organization who has buildings around the world with pictures and statues of us killing people for that old bad tempered scary guy on a throne who lives in heaven."

G: "To be fair, recently they think of Him as an all loving and forgiving God."

M: "That's not my point. My point is that these fantasies and their perpetrators should keep us out of it. Sometimes it is us who respond, yes. But we don't sell religion or belief systems. We simply guide you to your higher self-choices. Or we stop you from getting killed in accidents that were not meant to kill you but could. If anyone reading this had one of us telling you to get back to God, or Jesus… who's a great guy by the way, know that we mean your higher self or Christ consciousness. Not some external character whom you are not related to."

IB: "But my grandma told me Gabriel was an Archangel who looked after kids, and the picture I had was bought at the local Catholic church. And here you are…"

They both looked at me. If one could express a sigh and roll eye in a simple look, that's what they were doing. Except neither of them sighed or rolled their eyes.

I could feel a push to experience rather than listen. It was super strong, and I could also feel my resistance to it. My resistance won, and we stayed in the cabin sitting around the table drinking tea.

M: "How is she doing that?"

G: "I don't know."

I sensed Michael moving quickly toward me, pulling out a flaming sword and putting it against my neck, at the same time pushing my head with his left hand against the couch so I could not move. His eyes no longer human, but infinite and fiery. It reminded me of another question I had for them.

IB: "So… Lucifer. Is he your brother too? Is he an angel?"

I got a very powerful feeling that Michael was done playing games and he was not going to pretend to be interested in conversing with me anymore. He really wasn't. I felt a strong demand to show myself, to stop this charade and show my true form.

G: "Michael."

M: "Enough brother. This creature is not human. And you are being influenced by it. Influencing all of us in turn."

It came out of nowhere, deep inside me somewhere, but it was strong and pissed off. Yet controlled. A feeling of power and authority. My body felt as though it became solid, strong, stronger than Michael's. I gently pulled up my hand, grabbed his sword hand and pushed it away from me. I felt deep love and compassion for Michael, but firmly sent him an experience of "enough with the aggressive behavior, I won't put up with it anymore."

Michael struggled against it for a while, maybe an eternity, or a few seconds. Hard to tell. Then his aggression, sword and fiery eyes retreated and he was back to being just a big powerful man again.

M: "I told you she wasn't human."

Michael was looking at Gabriel, who in turn was looking at me.

IB: "I am only human. I've never had an incarnation in any other form. That humans are the creators of the universe is not just a theory. Just because most of us have chosen to forget it, and pretend to be helpless characters in a larger cosmic play, doesn't mean we have lost our capacity to control our own creation. If there is a difference between a lot of other people and myself, it would be that I have a knowing and awareness that we do create the universe around us moment to moment, and that without agreement, nothing can happen to us. It's not just a theory, it's real. And I'm not the only one who knows this or practices it. There are countless others out there who know it too. We don't use it much because it takes a lot to push against the collective agreement which has humanity playing with low vibrational rules."

M: "A lot of what?"

IB: "I would say a lot of desire. By default we are careful and mindful of the game others play. So pushing against those games is not something we often do. Humans don't often push their will onto others in large degrees. We are more prone to convince others, or trick them, into playing our games. Sometimes the convincing is by showing ourselves to be stronger than the other players and convincing them that we are stronger and that they have to do our bidding. But no one is stronger than another when it comes to choosing their personal experience."

M: "You call yourself human. You have human form, and a human life with relationships, children, a job, friends, dramas and pleasures. Yet, I know you are not human. No human can push me to stand down like that."

IB: "You speak a lot about us humans being God. You talk about us being the creators of the universe, yet when one of us shows you it is true, you say we are not human."

I felt a definite shift in Michael's energy. It went from aggression to servitude. From attack to guardianship. He stood up for a moment and then kneeled in front of me and lowered his head.

It was a sign of respect and a promise of no more aggression. Also, unconditional trust that I would not harm him. I was about to say something but instead I felt myself sit forward and a couple of thin brilliant white wings came out of my back and flexed a few times. They had bling.

Gabriel smiled. Michael looked up, examined them closely, patted me on the head and sat back down on his chair. Gabriel stood up and put out the embers on the couch that Michael's sword had burned into it.

M: "The wings are very pretty. And deadly."

I looked back at my wings and saw that the feathers were actually razor sharp blades. I didn't like that very much and instantly they turned into silky soft feathers. I flexed them a few more times, wondering what was happening or why they had appeared. I saw my kitten Theo become very interested in them, so I knew it wasn't simply a mental projection, they were in the third dimensional reality.

G: "It's very hard to relate to you Inelia. One moment you are an ocean of wisdom, knowledge and power, the next you are totally innocent and unknowing. Like a child. I think the best way for us to communicate with you is to remove our doubt and suspicions and take you moment to moment as you express yourself to be. You are quite literal, we are used to layers upon layers of expressions meaning other things or intents when relating to human beings."

Gabriel said this to me, but while looking at Michael.

M: "The wings are an expression of our intent and energy moment to moment. They are a different body, like you have an emotional body for example, we have wings. We have an emotional body too. And no, just because you have wings doesn't mean you are necessarily an angel."

G: "Just like many creatures have a physical body, or an emotional body, many creatures also have bodies that outwardly appear like wings."

IB: "I have definitely perceived wings on other people, almost have seen them with my physical eyes. But never solid like these ones."

When I stated that, I remembered yet another question I had for them. But felt it was probably better to leave it for the next time we met. I also felt that would not be for a while. There was a lot to absorb and process before our next meeting. I took up my notepad and wrote the question so I would not forget it again: "Can angels be born as human beings?"

As I thought about this, I stretched my wings out, it felt really, really good. It reminded me of the day at the beach, but then I was in an my astral body, this was my physical body. I could see the bling on the wings going crazy. But how come I had wings now? Could other people see them? And why did Michael pat me on the head like that when he saw them?

M: "Wings can't lie. In other words, they are a true expression of the being and their intent. Humans do have them, but mostly they are like an energy body in them. Us too, but we can express them physically at will. Like we can express physical bodies like these."

He pointed at himself and Gabriel.

G: "It appears that you have learned how to express your wings physically by seeing how we do it."

IB: "That resonates. Yes, thank you. What do my wings tell you about me?"

G: "How do you feel about them?"

IB: "Well, I think they are beautiful, delicate looking, super pure and bright, fun. I also see that they are deadly and extremely powerful.

Almost like their beauty and fun is so obvious that it's easy to forget they are deadly. Yet they seem delicate somehow. And playful."

Michael and Gabriel nodded.

I was about to say I am not deadly, but then remembered what had just happened with Michael and the power that I had become in that moment. I wondered why power had to be expressed in the ability to destroy or kill… the word deadly, the razor sharp metallic feathers. It didn't make sense to me. But when I had held Michael's sword away, I knew his response had been to destroy me. And my response was, "I can destroy you but choose for you to live. Stop attacking me." That's when I got a glimpse of an answer. We humans are not just creators, but can destroy too. When we create a new reality, we destroy a reality created by another. The power to destroy is as strong as the power to create in the human person. But destruction is not the same as power over others, inflicting of pain and suffering, or feeding off the fear of others. That has to do with something else entirely. Our ability to destroy has to do with dissolving what was there before, so the new can be born. One can't have a new paradigm where the old one still exists, for example. We destroy the illusions, or creations of separation, to step into a unified consciousness of reality. We destroy the ability of others to hurt us not by hurting them back or destroying them, but by simply stopping them from hurting us. By refusing to be hurt by them. We can also stop another's creation impinging in our own by dissolving them from our field.

Michael reached over and gently touched my arm. I cringed away from him. He put up his hand to show no aggression was meant and pulled back slowly.

M: "I will not hurt you."

IB: "I know. Sorry, I find it difficult to trust. It's one thing to be able to stop you hurting me, but another to expect not to be hurt by you."

Michael nodded and looked away. I felt he understood.

IB: "It's not just you. I feel that way about everyone. It's strange. From one perspective, when I am in a more expanded state of awareness, I am open and able to accept any being in my field. No judgment, no fear, no engagement but of the highest vibrational frequency. But when I am in a regular state of mind, I am vulnerable to pain and negative influence. I never expect to be attacked or hurt, but often am. This makes me cringe at the touch of others, and suspicious of any interaction they might want to have with me. It's a reaction of existence in the old paradigm, where power over others, and the use of other's power for personal satisfaction is paramount. I feel the power in me, and in my life many have tried to manipulate it or destroy it. And that's not unique to me. I have seen other very powerful people of pure intent be hijacked and used due to the simple fact that they would never suspect such behavior from another. Also attacked relentlessly. Now my smaller self has grown to be wary and untrusting."

M: "I apologize. I was no better than what you have described. Instead of trusting what I saw, as my brother has, I suspected you to be lying, using and manipulating us. It is difficult for me to accept what I can see with my own eyes and senses. I too have been used in the past."

IB: "Religions?"

M: "One might say that. On a small scale, yes. But my trust and love have been used to destroy entire worlds. Now my suspicion was used to try to destroy you."

IB: "Used by whom?"

M: "My own righteousness I suspect. Now my connection to you is damaged. You came to me open hearted and filled with wonder. I came to you wielding a sword and willing to kill you."

IB: "Yeah, not exactly what one might expect from an angel, huh?"

G: "You should see the paintings of Michael at the Vatican in Rome, then you would totally expect that behavior from him."

IB: "Back to religion then."

Gabriel and I smiled, but Michael did not.

M: "I can see, sense and feel that you are indeed human. But at the same time, I know that you are not. I'm sorry, I can accept that you believe you are human, that you express yourself as a human being. But I know you are different. And I can also sense, feel, and know that you don't know it."

IB: "I feel like we are going round in circles. I want to explore your view, I really do. But exploring what I am, what my experience here on this planet has been, and what capacities I have I don't think will help anyone. There is a tendency for people to project authority onto others, and also to use the fact that I'm different to them to validate their inability to move past their pain and suffering, or move out of the lower vibrational games they are playing. So, if I was to express what I have experienced here on this planet, or what my higher self or even smaller self feel like, that story might become the focus of attention, when the focus really should be in people becoming empowered in themselves and moving past all stories."

G: "We've had this conversation already."

IB: "Yes, we have."

M: "I think you are doing a wonderful job of it. I can sense and feel you are holding back, but also your… well… ignorance stops you from holding back too. I can sense and feel many people reading these words and knowing themselves to be holding back so that they don't get punished in some way, or used by others to validate pain and suffering. Fear is a strong motivator. Even holding back is useful when expressed honestly."

I nodded. I guess at the end of the day, my desire to stay hidden was best expressed as fear. I made a mental note to do the fear processing exercise on it.

My wings folded back and seemed to vanish into my body. I then also understood that the expression of those wings had been directly related to my desire to communicate with Michael. I remembered a knowing that is now well established in our race, that to manifest quickly, one's desire, or emotion of what something feels like, is the fastest way to manifest the end result. I deeply desired to communicate my nature to Michael, and felt open and willing, plus felt that I could and had communicated with him. And the wings appeared. A form of communication that could not be manipulated and that he understood completely. It felt like something important had been accomplished.

Michael was looking at me, his eyes were now deep oceans that reminded me of dolphins and whales. At the same time, they were fiery pits that could burn anything or anyone into nonexistence. I slowly opened my energy field and awareness to him, and felt him doing the same. The entire world, the universe and all time past present and future turned to pure, unconditional love. And it was OK to be, exist and express fully to ourselves and each other. No manipulation, judgment or punishment was possible in that expression or experience. A tear appeared in the corner of his eye, and rolled slowly down his cheek.

A few hours later, as I sat going through my notes, Larry walked in from his daily chores, he came over and read through what I had written down so far. "They didn't answer any of the questions." he said. I looked back and reviewed the conversation that day, and saw all the questions answered in full. I wondered why Larry's interpretation of the events contained no answers, and wondered if that was going to be the experience of everyone else who read this book.

"What happened to the couch?" he said as he looked over at the burn marks.

"Michael happened to the couch."

Chapter Six

It was three months before we met again. And I could say it was because Larry and I got busy with life, but the truth is that the incident with Michael had a deep effect on me. I'm not the nicest person on the planet by any means, and know that any negative situation we may find ourselves in has been opened by ourselves through programs, firewalls, beliefs or fears.

Sometimes a being will come at us at their frequency or with their baggage and we are able to deflect the attack through conscious awareness. But the attack still came. And that was what bothered me.

Many times in my life I have had the situation where I would be completely open to someone who would then turn and attack for what appeared to be no reason what so ever. I know that with Michael he could sense I was holding back, and the amount of awareness I had of him and his kind, the mutual effect our conversations were having on Gabriel and my approach to conversation being literal and not the regular beat around the bush type communication he was used to, put up all his red flags to the degree of going for the kill. Or at least threatening to. I was never in any danger, but what bothered me was the fact that he had attacked me.

My feelings were hurt and my confidence was shattered.

At the time, as I was in an expanded state of awareness, the incident was just an incident and there wasn't any judgment of it. And when I saw the blocks and opened myself to him, and he did the same, there was the ability to connect, get to know and expand into each other's awareness. The base energy was love. And that energy was pure, unadulterated, powerful and sincere. In that connection, he saw something that affected him deeply.

During public events, or even private meetings, where I am in an expanded state of awareness, I will connect with individuals in what I call a state of allowance. In that field, the highest possible vibrational frequency, they are allowed to exist in their full expression through time and space. No judgment, analysis, low frequency thoughts or connections. If they are also in an expanded state of awareness, they will have strong visions and perceptions. Sometimes these visions and perceptions are interpreted by them to be expressions of me. It is actually a mirror of themselves and their highest reachable potential at that moment in time.

It felt to me that that was what happened when Michael and I connected. He saw something that moved him deeply and gave him a very deep understanding. But I was not privy to what it was or what it meant to him, because it was not for me to see or know.

But when I got back to my smaller egoic self, all that expanded awareness and perception went away and what was left was a feeling of physical shock, betrayal of trust and fear at being attacked. Especially by an angel! Yes, he is clearly depicted in many cultures as being ruthless and deadly, but I grew up thinking of all angels as benign, loving, helpful, trustworthy, caring, guides and protectors.

Sharing this with you does not paint me in the best light. But it's what happened. And I did process my fear and all the other low frequency emotions and thoughts around it, but it took three months to get through it to the degree that I was open enough to see them again. If you are familiar with my work you will know that I teach to only process stuff for twenty percent of the day, and the rest to spend it in joyful and inspirational activities. So taking three months to process a traumatic incident like this is quite normal.

After three months it wasn't actually me who instigated the next visit. If it was up to me, it would probably have taken several years to meet with them again.

No. It was Gabriel. I was busy cleaning the leaves from the front porch when I saw him walking down the drive. The moment I saw him he stopped and waved. I realized he needed to be invited, so waved him over.

Sixth Interview

IB: "How did you get here? I thought you couldn't find me unless I called you."

G: "I searched, "Neah Bay", on the internet. Then walked around for a few days looking for you. A few months actually. Today I saw this property appear out of nowhere, so here I am and here you are."

IB: "Wow. That is fascinating."

G: "We need to talk."

IB: "OK. Do come in, Larry is out fishing for the next few days. Are you hungry? He left some spaghetti ready made."

G: "Spaghetti sounds perfect."

We went straight to the kitchen and I served us both some pasta. I got my recorder, then sat with him at the kitchen table. At first we just sat there eating. I offered him something to drink, fresh water was his drink of choice.

G: "Thank you for being willing to be found."

IB: "To tell the truth I didn't consciously choose to be found. But I suppose I do feel better now."

G: "What happened? Why did you stop calling me?"

IB: "Well, here's the thing. My life hasn't really been that easy. I don't talk about it much but there have been a lot of people trying to kill me or destroy me from the time I was conceived. So being attacked is nothing new. There have also been people who have loved and supported me of course, I'm not saying it has all been bad.

To me, writing is one of the greatest joys I have in life. I love writing. And to me it's something that's inspiring and a way to channel Divine Eternal energy, Source energy, into the human collective. But twice now, during the writing of these interview books, I have been attacked quite seriously by the interviewee.

With the previous interview I knew going in that it might be dangerous. I was dealing with a human assassin that had been programmed by the government. It was kind of inevitable that she would get triggered at some point and lash out. But this time I was dealing with angels.

You Gabriel have been exactly how I felt angels to be. You are very loving, open and you don't have any doubts or fears. Your openness is all encompassing. Spending time with you has been inspirational, informational, and truly an awareness expanding experience. But when Michael attacked me, it became not worth the effort. It was a shock. I expected more of you guys, angels I mean. You have such expanded awareness and have seen so much of the universe. There was no way I would ever think that one of you would feel the need to threaten me or try to kill me. I mean, you are angels!

Anyway, I'm no longer willing to be attacked by interviewees just to get these interviews out there into the world. So, I have reviewed the situation and decided to shelve the Interview Series. I'm writing a novel about the Anunnaki now, based on real events and people but without the need to interact directly with them in any way or form. OK, maybe some small interactions, but always from a distance."

G: "I do understand. What I witnessed was from that larger perception, I could see you were never in any danger. But if I look at it from the viewpoint of a regular person, it is something I should never have allowed to happen. I am responsible for this, I knew what my brother was feeling and I could have stopped it. I am so sorry. It is difficult for me to see you as a regular person.

You also have to know that although we do see a lot more than people do, and have lived and travelled extensively through the universe, every situation and every person is unique. Yes, there are patterns that we see repeated within species, and we know how to deal with those. But with the aspects of a being that is unique to them, we don't know how to respond."

IB: "Oh, I am not playing the victim here, or the poor little human. Although, it probably does come through that way, huh? What I'm saying is that I choose to concentrate my energies in activities where I don't open myself to attack. I am fully aware that I am the common denominator here, and that if I hadn't been holding back, Michael would never have become suspicious. But yes, I am a regular person and do have fears and other low frequency emotions. My holding back was not a conscious choice. My flaws are my own and I'm a slow learner, so I'm not going to risk this unpleasantness and trauma anymore. My physical body does feel the trauma each and every time. And it's my job to protect her and give her a good and happy life. I'm sorry to disappoint but I'm pretty much done with interviewing people and other beings such as yourself."

Gabriel nodded and simply sat and we continued with our lunch.

G: "Can I ask you something?"

IB: "Yes, of course."

G: "Do you know where Michael is?"

IB: "No, why? Where is he?"

G: "We don't know. He vanished after the incident with you and we haven't been able to locate him."

In my mind I couldn't help thinking about all the Michael followers around the world wondering where he'd gone. I'd met a few of them, the followers, and they were so intense and mission driven. Of course, without checking with Michael there was no way to know if all the followers were receiving orders from him or some Michael lookalike. But, most of the ones I had met were indeed his followers. I could see and feel Michael's resonant energy signature in them. It was unmistakable. Righteousness was very much part of it, as was their sense of mission. I was about to make a joke of it, but as I looked at Gabriel I saw his face was serious and concerned.

G: "I was hoping he was with you."

IB: "Why on earth would you think that?"

G: "Because you both vanished from our view and awareness at the same time."

Whenever someone asks me an interesting question, I can't help the desire to find out the answer. Suddenly, my unwavering decision to not have anything more to do with angels and interviewees went out the door, and I felt my awareness expanding, scanning first the world, then the known universe. Searching for an energy signature I had come to know intimately. That of Michael.

G: "We did that already."

At Gabriel's words I tapped into the data gathered by his own collective as they scanned the universe for their brother. It was flawed. They were looking for his signature as it had been for probably billions of linear time years from our perspective. Not his signature now. As I was linked to Gabriel's collective consciousness, he was able to see my reasoning. As soon as he perceived that Michael's signature was slightly different now, we got a hit.

G: "He's not far. I knew he was with you. I just knew it."

I grabbed Gabriel's hand and took him to the back porch. I pointed to the ocean. Not too far from the beach a large gray whale jumped out of the water, twirled in midair and splashed back in. I laughed.

IB: "Dolphins and whales. He's a whale!"

A whale song went through my lungs, yes, we can hear them in our lungs, and I was overcome with an amazing desire to jump into the cold ocean. I looked over at Gabriel, and felt his heart expanding toward his brother.

IB: "Wait!"

It was too late, Gabriel was gone and in the distance I saw another whale join the first. I watched them play for a few hours, then went back indoors to clean up the dishes. After a while I reopened the angel interview files on my laptop. I thought about transcribing the day's short conversation but the desire to jump in the ocean was too great. I thought about going to the beach and swimming out to them, but my swimming skills leave a lot to be desired. My kitten Brad jumped on the laptop and closed all the open files. I kissed his fluffy little head and headed out to the beach.

As I reached the water's edge I could see Tsoo-Yess beach and Strawberry Rock in the distance. The memory of how we had transported to an alternative location while still in the body was now fresh in my mind. I realized there was no need to get in the water. I lay down on the sand, closed my eyes and reached toward Gabriel and Michael.

Suddenly I felt myself in the water. It was so fresh and cool, exhilarating. I looked around and found my entire body moving with me. Around me, inside of me and what felt like the entire universe was filled with whale song. I could hear it in every cell of my body. Yet, I wasn't a whale! I was a dolphin.

I swam toward the song, and can't exactly say I actually saw them, but clearly perceived two whales swimming and twirling in the water. Their bodies shone bright, light exuding out of them and lighting the ocean around them.

I swam toward the lights and felt it tingle and infuse my entire body. I laughed and heard beautiful dolphin sounds and clicks come out of me.

"How come I'm not a whale also?" I thought to myself. "Because a dolphin chose you." Came the response.

It suddenly occurred to me that we hadn't turned into whales and dolphins but that a dolphin and two whales were actually hosting us, allowing us to share their bodies. We were borrowing their bodies to a degree I never knew possible. This realization blew my mind and I found myself laying back on the beach in my own body again. The transfer was so quick I felt like I was beached and couldn't get up for what felt to be an eternity, my skin felt dry and hot too. I was wowed out by the experience and it took me a while to digest it all.

I felt someone help me sit up, and give me some water. I finally was able to open my eyes and saw Gabriel smiling happily at me.

G: "High sentience level animals impinge more on one's embodiment than simpler forms when you borrow into them. You will be back to normal in a few hours."

I nodded and drank some more water. Borrowing birds or trees was definitely a simpler and much more defined experience than this. Even becoming the simpler creatures was easier. The whale song still rang strong in my lungs.

IB: "Where's Michael?"

G: "He's not ready to go back to work just yet. He's fine. Happy. He's been keeping an eye on you all this time."

IB: "That's very interesting, I thought you guys couldn't find me if I didn't want you to."

G: "Well, yes, that's how it works normally, but apparently you left a door open for him. Maybe it was the connection you made after the incident. It's not easy to explain but I can see a trace of his frequency in you and a trace of yours in him."

IB: "I have been thinking about him and processing my physical body trauma. And did some more research on him too. I guess if I look deeper, I can actually feel him in my field. And sense that the connection never went away, but just a few hours ago I had no idea where he was or that the connection even existed."

G: "Energy connections, or cords, can be totally invisible to people. Humans mostly will only take notice of them when they affect them negatively."

IB: "Energy cords, I have so many questions about those."

G: "Let's get you back on your feet first."

I closed my eyes and got used to breathing into my own body again. The whale song, and the feeling of being hot and dry, beached, started to subside. Soon I felt the cool air touching my face, and heard the surf as it gently moved back and forth on the sand.

IB: "Do you do that a lot? Totally borrow into other animals like that without any awareness of your own body, or in your case no external body at all? And do you also borrow into people that way?

G: "To say we do it a lot is very subjective. We do it, but we don't spend a great deal of time using and controlling the bodies of other beings to that degree if that's what you mean. We never force it either, it's always a mutually agreed activity. We put out the request, and often someone or something will respond."

I started thinking about Michael, how different his energy felt. But then, as I connected more fully to him, I could see that what I saw to be playfulness and frolicking in the water, was in fact him on a mission. He had decided to stay in my invisible bubble to protect me. But also to observe me undetected. Yup, that was the Michael energy I was used to. Man on a mission. In the distance, I saw the whale come to the surface again, blowing out some air. As I tried to communicate with it, I felt that there was no way to use words anymore. It was all emotions and experiential telepathy. And the range of frequency, or even common denominators to share in order to converse were so different that it was impossible for me to have a linear conversation at all, let alone ask any questions.

Gabriel helped me to my feet and we walked back to the cabin.

Chapter Seven

The next day I felt revitalized and ready to continue with the Interview Series. I had some moments of personal doubt in that my interview skills had a lot to be desired. For example my list of questions was not shrinking at all. And I had taken the whole experience way too personally. But reviewing what I had already written, it felt to me that the important aspect was to share the experience of having a discourse with these individuals. Having settled that, I began to wonder about what questions to prioritize and insist on, so that some good data could be gathered from having direct access to these extraordinary beings.

I set up my recording equipment and note pads on the porch overlooking the ocean, and sent out a call for both Gabriel and Michael.

Gabriel arrived a few minutes later, he looked super happy and he had a real bounce in his step. Michael declined the invitation, he had found an area rich with plankton and wasn't going to miss out on it.

Seventh Interview

IB: "You look so happy today, care to share?"

G: "Have you ever wondered why humans are obsessed with evolving, evolution and expanding their experience of life? Even those who are not following a path of enlightenment are into bettering their lives somehow. Better career, better relationships, make sure their kids have a better life than they did. Not all obviously, but those who we can say are in a good path in life. Or why even we, angels, have a sense of wanting to know where we came from and step into expanded states of awareness? Have you wondered why the Anunnaki, for example, are obsessed with their physical evolution and territorial expansion?"

I looked down and my very well thought and prioritized list of questions and sighed.

IB: "Well, yes, of course I have wondered about that. Who hasn't? Didn't we talk about this already?"

G: "Have you also wondered about our, your species and mine, interconnectedness throughout linear time, and also the ways in which we relate and interconnect? And how come we do that with other species too? And I don't just mean whales, trees, birds and planetary entities, I mean other humanoid species throughout the physical universe and ultra-dimensional universe. We are all connected in our relationships to each other. We all serve a purpose in each other's existence and also a role therein. Have you wondered why?"

I closed my notepad with the questions in it.

IB: "No. That, I had not wondered about before. But it's a fascinating question."

G: "Have you wondered where all this is taking us?"

IB: "Kind of yes. I have wondered about the whole evolutionary journey concept and where it came from."

G: "Me too! We too... angels now wonder too. After the experience yesterday, the mutual sharing of the same experience but us being of different species got me thinking. And then I saw the whole pattern, I mean we saw the whole pattern. When there is a big question that comes up for one of us, an angel, we open the question for our entire collective to look at. And we did. And we saw a pattern. A pattern of interconnectedness and also a template, or path, of evolution. Evolution has been interpreted by different species, and individual groups within those species, and even individuals within those groups, differently.

But overall the frequency to pull us into evolution is the same one. It's a pull, or a push… or both, to grow, expand, evolve."

IB: "I can see it. Yes. Well, I can see it within my own human species for sure, but not so much with regard other species as I don't really have much experience with other species as my contact with them has been minimal. But I know you mentioned, and I felt, the pull to find out who your creator was and also the pull your species has to step out of your limitations."

G: "Did you know that other humanoid species are born into human physicality all the time? There are beings from just about every highly evolved humanoid race in the universe walking around in human form right now. And most of them don't even know it. They just go to work every morning, have a few drinks and watch TV at night, make more human bodies and then die without even a glimpse of where their soul came from. Some come in knowing they are from somewhere else, or have a mission to accomplish, some think they came here to learn lessons, or help the human species evolve. But those are just small interpretations of the larger picture."

IB: "What is the larger picture?"

G: "You don't see it?"

I looked. Nope, I could not see it.

G: "We are travelling! All of us. All the species who interconnect, exchange experiences, relate to each other, get involved in each other's stories, histories and business. And all are in some way or another obsessed with evolution or expansion whether of their souls, their species or their physical bodies or territories. We seem to be obsessed with travelling to the very same place. We all want to reach that place and none of us know where or what it is."

IB: "We are all in a journey together, to get somewhere, we all call it and interpret it as some sort of evolution, and we are using physicality to get there?"

G: "Yes!"

IB: "Why physicality though? It feels to me that is more to do with points of awareness, or souls, that are doing the journeying."

G: "When you look into someone's eyes, what do you see?"

IB: "I see an eternal divine, all knowing being. And yes, I have wondered why they think that they are evolving or learning. They know it all already. Or obsessed with getting somewhere, a new dimension or such, when they already are that dimension. They are everything, everywhere and every time."

G: "When you look into the eyes of a cat or a dog, what do you see?"

IB: "I see... well, sometimes I see just the animal. A pure, beautiful spark of life and awareness in animal form. But sometimes I see another soul or creature behind the eyes, a more aware one."

G: "When you see a disembodied human being, say someone astral travelling or remote viewing you, what do you see."

I wondered how he knew I could see those.

IB: "I see a spark of light, like a multi-winged butterfly made of pure light."

G: "When you see a disembodied dog or cat, what do you see?"

IB: "I see them, their body, but more transparent than what they look like in real life."

G: "Because their physical expression is themselves, but a human's is not. A human is involved in a lifelong borrowing of a body experience. They are not their body, yet the body cannot survive without them. They dictate the creation of that body into physical form, and also the shape and look of that body, but they are not the body. The body is a different creature altogether."

IB: "Well, yes, that's true, I knew that already. I call it the human elemental body. It has its own awareness and consciousness."

G: "The human body was created from other physical expressions of intelligence, and then evolved by many species to host the soul expressions of many ultra-dimensional species. And while in human form, in other words, while existing within and as a human body, one of those souls is able to create physical reality."

IB: "And while in human form, they have all sorts of experiences and stories, which they then give meaning to and some will say it's evolution or learning."

G: "Yes. But it's not. How can it be? It's more like waves of souls take turns to be human and create physicality and that physicality is highly orchestrated for whatever wave is presently in the human bodies to have their chosen experiences. But what do those experiences really do if it's not about the personal growth of a soul that is already all there is? Do they distract, or maybe they do move us all into a new place or space, or time, that was not there before? Why do all humanoid species in the ultra-dimensional universe follow their interpretation of evolution so tirelessly?"

IB: "I see it all the time, a person totally obsessed with their personal evolution, becoming enlightened, becoming more than they are right now, and on a journey that is decades long, and when I look in their eyes I can clearly see that they are already the entire universe, Oneness. It has puzzled me endlessly."

I thought back at the experience we had had of stepping into a place or timeline where the human species had not separated from the environment and had not stopped functioning as a conscious collective. My thought was that perhaps they were not looking to evolve, as they already were aware of their unity. But as I tapped into that memory, I saw that they still had a collective sense of evolution and expansion. Even as individuals they had a sense of pushing the envelope of singular expression. I thought about the Anunnaki and their own obsession with physical expression and conquest. I thought about the angels and their quest to break their limitations. I thought about the other races I had met during my last interview book, and knew they were also into growing and expanding. I thought about the reptilians I had met during my life and felt their obsessive drive to perfection. I thought about the grays and their masters, and the Pleiadians, the Lemurians, the Syrians, the creatures we call fairies and elves, the elemental shamans who live near the Makah Reservation. I thought about the Sasquatch.

IB: "It's the core animating energy of all species I am familiar with except the Sasquatch. They feel complete somehow, not into evolution. The closest energy would be survival through time and space. I guess that could be interpreted as evolving, or travelling too."

G: "Yes, exactly. The core animating energy. What animates us. What makes us go forth in linear time, and outside of it too is embodied by different humanoid species in evolution or survival of some kind."

IB: "Gabriel?"

G: "Yes?"

IB: "What if we are not journeying somewhere, because we are all time and we are all space. What if we are in fact carrying something or someone to a destination?"

Gabriel went quiet for a while.

IB: "Our own perception limits our awareness and our interpretation of what we see. But what if physicality is a sentient being? What if time is a sentient being? Would we not be perfect vessels to carry them into a destination, or maybe even carry them into existence or allow them to persist through time and space?"

I could sense that the thoughts and observations were moving out of my human concept of understanding the universe, or even interpreting it. And that what I was now seeing, which was at the edge of it, would be very difficult to express in words, or even in experiential telepathy directly into Gabriel's collective. Gabriel was still deep in thought.

IB: "A cat or a dog, or a tree, never asks - why am I here? - And I think that's part of the answer. A cat or a dog or a tree never meditates to reach heightened states of awareness. It never looks in the mirror and judges its shape and form. It never chooses a mate to improve his or her species growth in evolution. Yes to survive, but not to evolve. When we look at fossils of birds, snails, trees, or animals, they mostly look identical today to what they did millions of years ago. And studying their environment shows us that their lifestyle and form of survival is still the same. When we look at humanity or humans just fifty years ago, we are not only physically different than we were then, but also our expression and life in the environment is radically different. We take cats and dogs and purposely choose their mates to improve their species in temperament and looks. We have been genetically guiding plants and animals to better serve our own survival. And now that we have the technology, we are bypassing the whole mating aspect of animals and plants and altering and mixing DNA to get better results for ourselves. We are even involved in the physical enhancement of humans through genetic alteration. You should see the stuff humans have done with reptilian technology at the Dulce base in New Mexico. It's horrific. Yet they do it because they think they are improving our species evolution, survival, conquest, and capacity to expand into the universe."

I was aware that we, humans, had been involved in genetically altering our own physical bodies since we had gotten our hands on technology that made it possible decades earlier, and was also highly aware that the Dulce underground base was not the only location where this was happening, but it was the location I had had most exposure to. As a child I had been taken there, and I had spent many years going back to it on a regular basis. So I knew the nature and the levels to which we were capable of going for the - evolution - of our species.

We were getting very close to an answer, or better expressed, we were getting very close to asking the right question. At the same time I could feel my attention and awareness struggling to stay focused on the topic. My mind started wandering into different directions and simpler questions came up for me to ask. I started feeling foggy and sleepy. I rubbed my eyes.

G: "I feel it too. Almost like the veil closing in on us. Let's go for a walk."

We walked through the woods on a deer trail. Around us the entire universe seemed alive and buzzing. Trees chatting to each other, insects getting excited at our presence, birds and rabbits coming into the trail to take a look before flying or hopping away. It was all so alive, even the rocks sparkled with knowing.

IB: "You know Gabriel, we don't often think of your kind as wanting or being driven to evolve or grow. We think of you as all knowing, static, unchanging. Even the story with Lucifer is one told of something that happened a long time ago and due to the fact that your people could not become more than you already are. This is so different to what I have seen of you. You are indeed explorers of worlds, universes and dimensions. You are indeed seeking answers and ways to break through the limits of your perception and existence."

G: "It's one of those things humans do, they project all their authority onto anyone or anything that they feel knows better than them. But that's just a DNA program. And as such, it can be removed by intent."

IB: "Yes, often I've been a passenger in a car and the driver gets lost, so they start following the car in front thinking they know the way. The fact that the driver in front knows the way to where they are going, but not where we are going seems to be irrelevant. Also, maybe the driver in front is also lost? The same pattern is seen when certain keywords are used in press releases and such. And when people channel information from other entities or species, often the audience will take everything they hear as gospel."

G: "So, there is a pattern to evolve, grow, become more, make more bodies, and also to be led, guided, driven in a direction by someone or something else."

IB: "Yes, creators who are told what to create and where to go. Good point."

We got to larger trail leading deeper into the forest and decided to go ahead and explore it.

IB: "There are other common denominators too, so far we have evolution, multiplying the species through bodies or territory, and we also have connection. We humans are pretty much obsessed with connecting with another, a special one, our higher self, our guides, our Source, our land, our planet, and even our animals and trees, oceans and such. There is a drive to reconnect that flows through just about everyone. There are books written about people who are isolated from other people on islands and such and they go crazy. One of the biggest punishments in human jails or dictatorship systems is solitary confinement and also exile. When you took me to that time or place where humans had not disconnected from each other, or their environment, the one where religion never was invented, my sense of self, or being, felt complete."

G: "We are also connected to each other, and we do value our connection to other species and our roles within their experience very much."

IB: "I was just thinking that even within the paradigm of light dark, or victim aggressor, there are patterns, loops and deep connections between the players. So, interconnectedness is not just high vibrational frequency. It goes beyond frequency and is a stable characteristic of our existence."

G: "I can pretty much say that connectivity and connection is a common denominator with every species we deal with."

IB: "Of course if there was a species that didn't care for connection, we wouldn't know about it as we wouldn't have any interaction with them. They would be invisible to us."

G: "Very true."

My mind was racing and I started feeling somewhat overloaded with information. We came to a clearing in the woods, and decided to find a dry spot to sit on. I really wanted to remember the common denominators we had with other species. I had a feeling that once we looked at all of them, we would be able to come to an answer as to the whole nonsensical stories we humans told each other about evolving and growing.

IB: "I think it has to do with physical bodies."

G: "But many of the species we deal with don't have physical bodies. Some do, but the great majority do not exist within this type of physical density."

IB: "By physical I guess I mean of expression within matter. And matter is made of energy. So, energetically expressed? Even a soul is a body in a way."

G: "Ah yes. I understand what you mean now. Well, there are two main types of incarnations. One, like we have already discussed which humans are part of, where the physical body and the soul are separate entities which are intimately codependent in their physical experience. If we think of just the soul as a being, which it is, it also has a physicality in the form of a very subtle energy point. Yet, the soul itself, when fully awake, doesn't pursue an evolutionary process."

IB: "The question then is, what does it pursue, and why does it ever exist in a state that is not awake. Why does it choose to fall asleep? What is the real purpose of having physical experiences for a soul if it already has had physical experience? The soul is the physical expression and the experience and the time and place it exists in. Ultimately it is the entire awareness of existence, all consciousness, all energy that ever exists or existed, all time, everything so why would it choose to be less, and then pretend to be expanding to more?"

G: "Well, now we are moving more towards the direction of an awareness of being Oneness rather than a soul."

IB: "What is the difference?"

G: "I can relate it to how I experience life. I am both a singular soul being, who can morph and change shape and physical essence at a soul level. I am the physical expression that you can see right now, there is no separate body entity. When I borrow into a whale, I am not the whale at a soul level. I am me, the whale is its own entity, and we are just sharing each other's senses and lives for a short while. When it comes to my species, I am not *part* of my species, I AM my species. I am my collective consciousness. If we move past the collective, then I am all species, all time, all matter, all souls."

IB: "I heard that angels don't have souls."

G: "We don't *have* souls. We ARE souls. Humans are a combination of a soul and a physical body which is its own entity. The soul has its own trajectory of experience and the body has its own trajectory of experience. The soul can live without the human body, and does. The human body cannot live without the soul, it decomposes and returns to a state of potential. A bit like a disembodied bundle of information which then finds another point to manifest at. Not unlike a soul in many ways."

IB: "It is so strange that we would join physical bodies to have a physical experience as souls, when you for example can create physical bodies at will. Why can't we express physically as a soul entity like you can?"

G: "I think it's related to reality creation. The very nature of physical experience at this level of density is, or I should say the existence of physical expression at this density is created by a larger intelligence. Choreographed, one might say, by the intelligence of collectives. It feels to me that in order for the physical to have shape and form, it needs structure. If one thinks of DNA, for example. The building data of sentient physical expression and existence. It expresses itself very fluidly. The sense that it is solid, or that it is difficult to change, is but an illusion. DNA is just data, but an intelligence chooses what data within it is used at a material level."

IB: "Oh! Maybe it is just about DNA. When I look into DNA I see a vast ultra-dimensional energy thing. Links and data flowing in and out of dimensions, time and space."

G: "That's an accurate observation. And it might actually be an important clue as to what the evolutionary and expansion journey is all about."

IB: "Why do you say that?"

He picked up a stick from the ground and looked at it intensely. Then he peeled a bit of bark off it, and handed it to me.

G: "Think about it. This DNA, the DNA in that bit of bark, is no different to the DNA of the fingers that are holding it."

I looked at the piece of bark and at my fingers. They felt radically different. Yet, they were indeed made not just of the same atoms and electrons, neutrons, energy, but their data bundles were only very slightly different from each other. Or I should say, the expression of the data was different, the data itself was identical.

IB: "Data."

I smiled. Gabriel looked at me, waiting for me to say more.

IB: "The common denominator Gabriel, it's all data! Think about it. What happens when we have an experience, we bundle it into packets of data and call it memories. What happens when we have an emotion, it's data processing and interpretation. The physical world is made of bundles of data. The concept of living in a Matrix is not new, it's quite ancient actually. An artificial reality, a dream, ran by an artificial intelligence, which we might say is our collective awareness, or maybe some other intelligence. And the only thing, the only point to it that is readily visible is the existence of the matrix itself, the carrying or creation moment to moment of the data itself. The bundles of data existing as a coherent whole. But why would we do that? Why would we bother? Why would we be willing to remove our expanded awareness of who and what we are so quickly and thoroughly just to keep the matrix alive?"

I took Gabriel's hand and looked to see his DNA. I could not sense any DNA. It really felt that he was not real, like he was a system of feedbacks that showed a person in front of me, and a hand that was solid. All created out of awareness, or intelligence, or light, but it felt more like awareness than data. His hand started vanishing in front of me. We both looked at it in surprise.

G: "Well... that's unexpected."

I closed my eyes, strongly disagreeing to Gabriel's hand being transparent, I felt a fear that he would disappear altogether. I processed that fear, knew it was always possible for me to see him, opened my eyes again, and saw he was still there, his hand back to a regular looking solid, real hand.

We both laughed, then spent the next half hour trying to remember what we'd been talking about. I reached into my pocket and saw my phone had been recording our conversation all along. With a sigh of relief, we walked back to the cabin, joking about what might be in the recording.

Chapter Eight

If you are reading this chapter and can't remember what was discussed in the previous chapter, it's because the topic is one of those that we are programmed to remove from our awareness. The reason we remove it from our awareness is because it spoils the illusion of reality. In all my interview books, and sometimes during live conversations with friends, or show hosts, there is a moment when I cannot recall what we have been talking about. Often, the person with me will not recall what we talked about, or that we had even had a conversation, a day or two later.

The reason this happens is that we live within a collective consciousness. Our species, has evolved technology that can continuously scan and tap into every single thoughtform we have. When those thoughtforms are not compatible with the experience we have agreed to have with others, or for ourselves, the thoughtforms are removed from our memories.

There are ways to keep them. We can record all the conversations we have with interesting people, then listen to them over and over again until the memory sticks. We can read the chapter that blanks out on us in a book over and over until it sticks. We can intend, as we are reading, that we now want this information in our created reality. Then read it over and over again.

This capacity, and technology, can be used to steer us into a human reality that feels like it is out of our control. Yet, it really cannot control us or what we allow into our awareness. Not really. We might not remember having that conversation, and might not remember what was written in the previous chapter, but we do know that we are curious about it. We know we forgot it, and can take measures to remember it. We have a choice. We always have a choice.

I was thinking about all this when I felt Michael in my awareness. He was happy. He told me that he was going to go out of the area because his family needed a change of scenery and type of food.

IB: "Your family?"

Yes, his family, he answered, and I saw a family of whales in my mind.

Pondering his response, I remember the story of how Vishnu had incarnated as a pig. After a while Vishnu forgot his divinity and though he really was a pig. And that looking after his piglets was the most important thing in the world. Gods and Buddhas came to him and would whisper in his ear, "you are not a pig", but he was happy and content and stayed as a pig until dying. At which point, he remembered he was not a pig, but a God.

IB: "You are not a pig, Michael."

M: "Of course I'm not a pig. I'm a whale."

I smiled and let it go. If Gods could not convince Vishnu that he was a God and not a pig, I didn't have much of a chance convincing Michael he was not a whale but an angel. Plus it really felt like he was pulling my leg. I felt a big wink come my way. I giggled.

M: "Inelia, you are not a pig."

IB: "Of course I'm not a pig, I'm a human."

I knew we were joking and playing with the sense of who and what we are at any one time, but as I laughed at his response, it suddenly occurred to me that this conversation was very much related to the topic we had covered in the previous chapter. A God incarnated into the body of a pig and became convinced he was a pig, forgetting his divinity completely.

We incarnate into physical reality and completely forget where we came from, what we are, and why we incarnated into physical reality. Most of us feel and sense that this is a willing participation in doing something here, on this planet. Most of us have a strong sense of mission. Yet, some feel it is a trick or a prison. Whenever I look at it, it feels to me that it is more of a willingness to be tricked into a mission. An eternal divine, all knowing being cannot be tricked unless it purposely chooses a lower level of awareness for a while. And why would it do that.

Also, as I observed Michael in his new game, moving away from my awareness and from the area with his whale family, I sensed that there was a strong connection between enjoying the physical world and becoming addicted to it. I wondered if the physical reality was sentient, and needed souls to keep it alive and, well, real. To stay alive, it offered experiences and things that were rich in sensory stimulation. Everything we feel at a physical level is only felt here, it does not carry to the in-between lives place, or even to other realities we might encounter during out of the body experiences. It also occurred to me that we spend a lot of time out of the body, we sleep. And if we don't sleep, things go bad for us very fast. My thoughts came full circle to the meaning and importance we give life.

Without meaning and importance to their experience and existence, most people quickly die. I've seen it so many times as people work for decades at their job, they die a few days or weeks after they retire. Or when couples are close, they die from natural causes within days or weeks of each other. It is almost as though the relationship between the body and the soul can only be kept if the soul believes it has a purpose here and the belief that what it does or experiences is important. And what more important than personal evolution, or the growth and survival of our families, tribes or nations?

Michael left my location and I wondered if he would become trapped in the whale body until that body died, or whether he would remove himself from it without losing perspective of what he truly was. I sensed that he had done this many times before, and as a multidimensional being, he could live and enjoy being a whale and also have the capacity to visit his followers and give them powerful and important missions to do on the planet at the same time.

There was a knock at the door. It was Gabriel.

Eighth Interview

IB: "Come in, it's open."

G: "Morning."

IB: "Good morning! How come Michael has so many followers and people that do his missions while you don't?"

G: "No cup of tea first?"

IB: "Oh, of course, I'll put the kettle on. But seriously, I have met Michael followers and channelers, and they are intense. And highly mission driven. Plus there are a lot of them all over the world. Did you know that Brussels, which is the seat of the European Union and many organizations that are actively pushing for the old paradigm, is filled with statues and churches dedicated to Michael?"

G: "Not all the followers are listening to Michael himself, there are other energies and entities pretending to be him. And like we discussed before, because of his warrior energy, and the fact that he reflects fear back to people who carry it, he has been used as a symbol of wrath."

IB: "He has a huge following though, and you don't. There are those who do indeed channel you, and follow you. But not to the same degree as they do Michael."

G: "I guess people prefer to embody and follow his fiery and protective energies than my more gentle and nurturing ones."

IB: "Can you tell us how to discern, how our readers can discern, what is really coming from you or Michael and what is another entity coming in pretending to be you?"

G: "Well, all I can say about that is that whomever is coming through is irrelevant. Whether the message really came in from Michael or myself, or some other entity is not important. What you need to look at is what the message is saying, what it is conveying both in essence, energy, and content."

IB: "I always distrust any message that use the words beloved, beloveds, dear one, or supreme creator, God, Jesus or other religion specific words."

G: "There are two things to keep in mind when you hear those words. One is that although your personal experience was somewhat unique when meeting Michael, most people feel his deep love and universal spirit of passion and protection for all living beings. As his thoughts, feelings and seeings come into the person who is channeling him, they get interpreted into the language the person speaks as well as the cultural and religious programming that person has. So, for example, the word *beloveds* expresses his love for the people who are listening. Indeed it is not a word he or I would use, but it is the sentiment we feel.

My advice would be if you want to start reading people's channelings, and not just those who channel Michael or I, aim to be more open, to have the willingness to get to the core of the message rather than the dogma or agendas the person might be carrying at a subconscious level.

But I do understand that it is a hard thing to do, to see a core energy or message when the person is telling you to go to your local church, give your power away, tell you to do as they say, or listen to what is being said because they know better than you, are all knowing or have the only true and real answers. Or tells you God is a man in heaven or a being that created you."

IB: "Yes, it's hard for me to read or listen to channelings these days. Most seem to have that type of energy in them. The one that expects the listener to give their power away, or ignore their own inner guidance. Sometimes they start right, and the information they channel for the first few years is really great. Then it goes sideways. Sometimes they have one very powerful gem, and then start talking absolute rubbish. And then I feel like I can't share that gem because people will automatically assume I am advising them to listen to the rubbish too."

G: "Yes, I have noticed that many people are very willing and ready to be led, to give their power away and follow someone blindly. But that's not from a place of subservience, although many religions have steered it that way. It is from a place of innocence and willingness to learn and grow. It also has to do with a DNA sequence that was integrated into the human body to basically follow the leader. Follow orders without question."

IB: "And we go back to the same topic, like looping back to the same questions. Why would an eternal, divine, all knowing being have the need to learn and grow, or even follow orders? And why do most people of a high frequency need to learn how to function and survive in negative and painful circumstances, why do they fall for the lies that tell them pain makes them better people when they arrived here pure of soul, intent and energy?"

G: "It does loop back to the start."

IB: "I think that the most important thing to remember is that pain and negativity are not necessary. They are simply distractions that stop people from expressing their essence and embodying a really high frequency vibration experience. We came here to help the human collective move away from the illusion and experience of pain and fear being necessary in any way or form. It seems to be a choice now, a general choice, that people have. To have an experience of life without fear or pain. Yet I can still strongly feel a resistance to that statement within the human collective. Even though all pain and fear does is to create more pain and fear. There is still a huge resistance to acknowledging the fact that pain and fear, as an existential basis, is useless. So much value is given to them. And that is another question I have for you. Who and what exactly needs pain and fear to be felt by us so much that they have created a whole planet filled with it and feeds us with it relentlessly through every channel of communication we have invented?"

G: "It's easy to fall into the thinking that humans are victims of another species who feeds on fear and pain. From a standpoint of no judgment, I see the human experience to be a range of frequencies and colors, vibrations. Many, many people are addicted to fear and pain. They are strong emotions and if misinterpreted in a certain way, it gives a person much meaning and purpose. Are there beings who feed on it? Yes. Also, for as long as a person has a life filled with fear and pain, they cannot step into their power, they cannot become fully enlightened about the reality they exist in, or their own essence. So, one might say that it is a self-feeding loop. Fear in itself creates more fear, creates a disempowered reality, creates addiction and willingness to do many things that go against one's principles or integrity. Add the follow the leader programs and you have a very pliable species of reality creators. Anyone who controls the fear, dictates what the species creates. And maybe it's just a way to stop people from exiting this reality. Maybe that's all that's important, and keeping them in a very narrow point of awareness is the only way."

IB: "When I was little, I put on my mom's high heel pumps. I was walking around the house with them on, they were huge on me, and it was hard to walk around. My dad saw me with them on said, 'don't start wearing high heels, they are no good during wars, you cannot run in them.' I looked at him for a while and said, 'I don't plan to be in any wars.' He responded, 'you cannot avoid wars, they come at you whether you choose them or not.' I thought about this. Then responded, 'well, if a war comes at me, I'll take the heels off and put on boots. But daddy, really, if a war comes, I prefer to die because I'm not really into wars.' He went into a long lecture about fighting for our rights and such. I think he missed the point. As it happened a war did come, but I was too young to either wear pumps or fight in it, or even die in it. Seriously though, who is behind the enormous amount of investment in money and time to create such suffering, pain and fear in our societies around the world? Wait, a follow the leader program?"

Gabriel looked at me, then at the table and started fidgeting with the salt and pepper, moving them back and forth.

G: "Did you forget our previous conversation?"

IB: "Yes. Well, kind of. I did. Yes."

I totally had… again!

IB: "I listened to it several times, until it stuck somewhat. But I can see now that you mention it, it was about evolution and the program to follow the leader in the human collective. It was about DNA, data, existing for existence sake and all of us being on a journey to get somewhere. From that perspective, shifting our reality from a painful and fearful experience to a happy, satisfying, and creative experience is kind of irrelevant. Except perhaps in that people are done with suffering and are bailing out of this reality, so a new, different reality needs to be created in order to have souls be willing and interested in entering it."

G: "I'm not so sure that the shifting of a reality, or embodying a new reality in one's life or body as a human being, to anchor it into this one, is relevant to the evolution part of the equation. Or the journey so many species are involved in. There are other races in the other expressions of Earth, and I do believe you met some of them, who have no concept of fear or suffering. Who have no concept or reality of power over others. Yet, they too are in an evolutionary process or process of expansion. I do think it has to do with keeping it interesting though."

IB: "During one of our conversations, you mentioned that you could see when a person veered off their chosen path and you went in to try to steer them back on their path. And also you mentioned that you could see when they made a big step in their right direction. You also talked about how you, as a species, only work with those who are moving in a direction of expansion of awareness and also high frequency vibrations."

Gabriel nodded.

IB: "I'm wondering now, about that. If evolution is not real, but a journey to get something else to a different place or time, why are angels involved in the moving of a divine eternal being into a more 'aware' or higher frequency vibrational state? I am also wondering why so many people who have incarnated into this human collective during the past few decades and who are here only to help it manifest a higher frequency vibration need help in their evolution in the first place? They are already evolved. The guidance I feel they do need is for reducing their suffering, as well as expressing their light in a safe and effective way so that the overall vibrational expression of the human race is a positive one. They don't need to evolve per se"

G: "It is better understood when we look at what a soul really is. How would you describe a soul?"

IB: "I see the soul to be a viewpoint. A point where the being can see, perceive, experience and express from. The awareness or observer behind the thoughts."

G: "From that description, would you say that the soul had a personality? A history? Or a trajectory?"

IB: "Well… no. it is simply an awareness point."

G: "Yes, I agree. I was wondering how you perceived a soul because I felt that your and my description of a soul were different, we were talking about different things. For me the soul is the first body. Just like a human looks out from his or her physical body, the awareness point looks out from a first body, one that is not physical but does contain all the memories, experiences, importances, personality traits and skills that the being chooses to carry through time and space. It is data, and how it's held together is through threads of importance, interest, and connection. This first body, or the bundle of information and data that the viewpoint chooses to wrap itself inside of, persists in all dimensions and lives. It is what animates the physical body of the human, and what expresses as physical in angels. It has a personality whereas a viewpoint, by definition, does not. From this perspective, one could say that the soul grows or evolves into a more complex and able body."

IB: "That explains a lot of things. One might even say that the first veil of forgetfulness is the point in time and space when the viewpoint identified itself with the soul body, or soul construct. One might say also that's the point when separation happened."

G: "Yesterday we were looking at the matrix construct of reality, and also the real reason behind the drive to evolve or expand being a vessel to carry something or someone to a destination. We also looked at the something being data itself. I can't help thinking that perhaps the first body, the soul, is key in this theory."

121

Gabriel looked at me for a few seconds and he looked puzzled.

G: "When I look at a being, they exist through time. Their soul construct persists and exists in linear, and nonlinear time. It really does not have an end or start point. When I look at you, your soul starts when you were born. That's the point it came into existence. And it exists from that point to all points, giving an illusion of eternity where eternity does not exist."

IB: "That would explain why I am not very attached to my personality, nor singular existence, and although I know I can learn stuff, I also know I am incapable of evolving. There is no interest in me to evolve, or survive. I also know that when the physical body dies, the 'I' that I am now, will dissolve into non-existence. When I have died in the past, it was another soul that held my viewpoint until I was returned into my physical body. It's an odd experience. I do have a soul construct, but it's brand new, and not permanent. It's necessary for, as you said, to animate the body but also necessary to be able to communicate and exist within the planet and the human collective."

G: "How big or small is your awareness point?"

IB: "It varies. It can be as big as the universe, or I should say it can be the universe, it can be Oneness, it can be the human collective, it can be just me, Inelia. Recently I've been able to be Inelia more effectively. But for most of my life, it was difficult to keep my viewpoint from a singular being perspective."

G: "Your physical body is not constant either. Not as constant as other people's. I was watching you while you interact with others, and I see your physical body appearing different to each person you are talking to, or are next to."

IB: "Yes, I've noticed that. It is also reflected in photos people take of me. Often I appear to look like them, or I look like the person I am sitting next to, or look like what the person taking the photo needs to address or look at in their own lives. In some photos I look angelic, in others I look demonic. In some I look like I'm 100 years old, and some I look like a teenager. It's frustrating because I want to look beautiful in all of them. A demonic expression doesn't do me any favors."

I pulled my hair back and rubbed my face with both hands. Gabriel laughed.

IB: "What's so funny?"

G: "It's just so disconcerting, one minute you are talking about something deep and filled with insight and wisdom, the next you are talking about looking pretty in photographs. I don't know. It just feels so opposite of each other."

IB: "Oh right. Wise people can't be vain or egotistical."

G: "Yes, something like that. It has more to do with perception of importances."

I thought about that for a while, *perception of importances*. Then remembered my priority list of questions I had in my notebook. I opened it up and, before we changed subjects yet again, I read the first question.

IB: "Are some humans angels incarnated in human form? Can angels be born as humans?"

G: "I won't pretend to know how that question is relevant or follows from our conversation, but I will answer it the best I can....

Yes."

I waited for Gabriel to say more, but he didn't. He looked over at my notepad, as if to ask for the next question on the list.

IB: "Wait just one minute mister. You can't just say 'yes' and not give details."

G: "But I answered the question. OK, what type of details do you want?"

I thought about this for a bit.

IB: "OK, tell me how that works, how does an angel decide to incarnate in a human body, why would they do that, what happens when they do, do they retain memory of being an angel, do other people know they are an angel, and what type of life do they lead once in a human body?

G: "Although we are and live primarily as a collective body... that's another type of body we exist as by the way, a collective soul body... so even though we live primarily as a collective body, or soul, we are also singular souls. Each angel has absolute power and control of the life they lead and the choices they make. As such, there have been cases of angels who have spent a lot of time with the human species through time and space, and who, for reasons of their own, decide to go native as it were. They decide to have an experience of being human. This could be mission based, or it could be to get a closer look at how things work, or it could be because they are curious as to what it feels like. Like most souls who incarnate into human form, they instantly forget who and what they are, and just like every other soul species that decides to incarnate in a human body, they instantly become human. The type of life they lead depends on how able they are in managing life on Earth. Other people rarely know they are talking to an incarnated angel, although sensitive or psychic people often do see it. This makes no difference to the angel's experience of being human, and often makes no difference to the people around them either. Personality-wise, if they survive, they do tend to become teachers, guides, healers and often become part of other people's physical entourage."

IB: "So their basic traits as angels continue on."

G: "In most cases, yes."

IB: "Do they get an entourage too?"

G: "Yes they do, and before you ask, yes, their entourage is mostly made up of angels."

IB: "Do you have an entourage?"

G: "Not as such. Angels, as well as other species that are connected to their collective, don't need entourages. We can be guided, supported and accompanied by the individuals in our collective as well as the collective as a whole."

IB: "That's fascinating. So we humans need entourages because we have disconnected ourselves from our collective and environment. I wonder if the entourage fulfills the role of a collective connection, or soul family?"

G: "That makes sense."

IB: "Do I personally know any incarnated angels or have I met any in my life?"

G: "Yes. Some are very close to you. But I would highly suggest that you either do not ask who they are, or if you do, don't publish their names or tell them they are angels. This could complicate things for them. When an incarnated angel is ready to know they are an angel, they find out in a very gentle way. If you try to force that knowledge onto them, or they get it from external sources, it can cause unnecessary difficulties."

I thought about this for a while and decided that I would not ask who they were. It would be pretty hard for me not to say anything to them, or not write about it.

IB: "I guess I don't want to know who they are. Right, that's the first question dealt with."

I read the next few questions and realized that we had already covered most of them during our other explorations. I crossed those off, and went onto the next unexplored question. I was on a roll.

IB: "One of the other things that have always puzzled me about this planet, and existing here, is that it is always consuming itself. Well, not the planet per se, but all the living animals, plants, viruses, bacteria, fish… if it lives, it's eating something or someone else to survive. Like an endless chain of consumption. Is this normal in the universe or is it particular to this planet only?"

G: "It is rather unique to this universe but not to this planet. It's interesting to watch, it seems to be a natural state for those entities that are expressions of their self, as we looked at before, such as cats and dogs and all the way to one cell entities. But for humans, as they are also a soul body, and they have the creative, physical reality manipulation, capacity, it's not necessary for them to consume living entities. At an extreme level of self-awareness and physical existence control, the person doesn't even need air or water to live. They don't even need a supportive environment for that matter. A completely awake human can live as comfortably in the middle of an active volcano as he or she can in outer space or their house."

That was a radical way to see things. I could understand the logical conclusion of deprogramming our dependency on food and even environment resulting in us being able to exist within all situations, we have all seen yogis walking on fire, or lying down on nails, but I could not conceive of it as something real or achievable for the rest of us. Then, a really interesting thought occurred to me.

IB: "What about linear time, or any time? Could a human exist outside of time and space altogether? I didn't do very well when I tried to step out of linear time a few months ago outside the restaurant."

Gabriel thought for a while. I knew he must be thinking of his own race's restrictions on their awareness and also their limitations to exist within the confines of time and space.

G: "Theoretically, yes. Deprogramming the physical body to follow the soul to other dimensions, outside of time and space, and survive or flourish there does remove the limits. But I can see the difficulties around this, particularly as the physical body was especially designed, or made, to live within linear time and a constant space. In a way, it is a way to keep a soul in linear time and anchored to one physical location. The physical body seems predisposed to stay put and does not like changes very much. Your own body and consciousness did indeed have difficulty stepping outside of linear time. But it's not impossible."

IB: "Yes, even moving too fast or not stable enough within linear time and space gives a lot of us motion sickness. A body reaction to trying to control being in a steady, stable, non-moving environment."

G: "I can sense that it is possible, but not met a human who has achieved it with any great success. And to think of it, not met an angel or other soul body species who has achieved it. Achieved movement and survival from all restrictive programs for movement or nourishment I mean."

IB: "Which reminds me, do you need nourishment or food of some sort when you are not expressed in a human body? Do angels eat?"

G: "We gain nourishment and energy from our Source. We don't ingest energy or matter from our environment or other beings."

IB: "How would you describe your Source?"

Gabriel drank some of his tea, and looked out of the window. After a while he looked back and nodded.

G: "I have to be articulate enough that my words don't get misinterpreted and hijacked into thinking there is one entity that created us all. The reason is that we do have a creator, but the word creator is not a person or one singular intelligence as such. If I talk about our Source, it's difficult to convey the experience of what that is to us with the vocabulary we hold."

He was silent again.

IB: "Instead of explaining it, why don't you describe to me the mechanics of how you exist or nourish yourself instead? What exactly do you do instead of eating?"

G: "That's a good idea. The way I would describe it is that when I feel low in energy, I would do an equivalent of closing my eyes… although we don't have eyes like you have eyes, we can lower our input of external information. I would lower the input of information that is coming in from my senses, and go to my core center. What you might call your heart center perhaps. There is a line of energy from our core to all of existence. Again, I am short of words. We are connected to a core of life, or core of existence. I simply sit there at that core for a while and I am soon full of energy, enough to manifest myself as a body with physicality of an energetic level. When I am in human form, the best way to maintain energy for me as a human is to eat and drink and breathe. I could maintain my human body in the same way as I do my angelic form, connecting to Source, but it would take longer for me as

I am not practiced in this. At the end of the day, all matter is basically energy. Chi. So how we absorb depends on what is easiest for us and what we want to do with that body."

IB: "I get a feeling that we could do that too. I mean humans, we humans could nourish ourselves by tapping into our Source energy or core."

G: "Yes, you can. Many already do."

IB: "I wonder if sun-gazing or prana breathing are ways, methods, that we use to make it possible. That it's not the sun or prana we are feeding from but actually our Source. And the methods are just ways for us to agree to it or comprehend it at a body level."

G: "You can absorb just about any type of energy to sustain the human body. Sun-gazing and prana breathing, are like eating. You take nourishment from your environment. It's a step in the right direction, but not exactly the same as simply tapping into your Source energy. One might say… again, that all is Source, so eating a steak or breathing in prana, or absorbing the energy from the sun… or tapping into one's Source, is all the same."

IB: "It is the same at the end of the day, but some of them limit us, and some of them don't. When we need to ingest food, and I know we talked about the social aspect of it before, we are dependent on having physical food to eat. This has created enormous dependency on a social system that enslaves people. I'm thinking that absorbing our nourishment from the sun traps us to this planetary system. Breathing in Prana makes us dependent on being able to breathe in. And then we start thinking about air and water. Which are not food, but have very strong and powerful functions in our physical existence. More than food actually. They makes us totally dependent on our planet. We die if we cannot exhale carbon dioxide, which we do by absorbing oxygen… which is used in our bodies to create the energy needed to do just about anything. Again, back to energy. Our bodies are also mostly water and we need to replace that water constantly during the day, with fresh water. Outside of our planet, water is a rare resource from what I understand. So we are basically trapped here until the day we can morph our bodies into not being dependent on food, water and oxygen."

G: "Those are interesting thoughts and conclusions. One has to remember that the human body is indeed an earth entity, but the soul is not. The soul is capable of manifesting itself as a body independently of a human body. So there is no reality to being trapped. Yes, at the moment if you want your human body to stay alive in this dimension and reality, you need to come back to it regularly, every day if possible, and feed it, water it and keep it breathing."

Something attracted my attention in what Gabriel said just then, so I stopped my train of thought and focused on what he had just said.

IB: "The words you used, 'you need to come back to it regularly, every day if possible,' are you referring to sleeping at night?"

G: "Yes. Every night you leave your body. The dreams and other experiences you remember happen in a few minutes or seconds as you enter your body again. But most of the time you are asleep, your soul is elsewhere."

IB: "Where do we go?"

G: "What I have seen is that the soul has its own experience and often does not share it with your conscious awareness as a human person. When you are children, there seems to be less of a distinction between the life you lead in the body and the life you lead outside of the body. But as you grow older, the two get divided."

IB: "But where do we go? What does the soul do that doesn't involve the body"

G: "Often it will explore and travel the Earth, sometimes it goes to other dimensions and other planets. Sometimes it just goes back to their place of origin, the species they first expressed as matter with. Many souls have multiple bodies in multiple dimensions and planets and they have experiences in those. With some individuals, their soul goes back to Source every night."

IB: "How can we tell what our soul is doing?"

G: "You can begin with having an intent to be consciously aware of what your soul is doing during the night. You can also intend what you want your soul to do at night. But I have to warn you, you are the one who chooses to forget that experience, and it is probably so you can continue this one, the embodied in a human body one, without interruption."

IB: "Like a game spoiler if we remember?"

G: "Yes."

IB: "Do those who go back to Source have a better understanding of life?"

G: "When having a daily human experience, most people are not aware of their experience during sleep. Although it does have an effect on their overall frequency vibration, whether they have a better understanding of life is too subjective to quantify. If their source is of a high frequency one, they do tend to be happier in daily life."

IB: "Something else that happens that we don't remember when we come back or wake up, is abductions by aliens. Sometimes the abductions are by our own government. How is it possible that they can wipe our memories like that, and if it is us choosing not to remember, why would we do that? I cannot think of any reason why I would intentionally forget being taken by the government to be tested and probed. Or by aliens for that matter."

G: "When a person is taken, their body is taken too. The memories are artificially repressed, but do exist. The memories can be regained through hypnosis or regression therapy, but often this brings in a lot confusion because the entire experience is remembered as subjective. Not quite real. This is the effect of the frequencies and sometimes drugs that are used to suppress the experience. It is often possible because the person subconsciously desires the experience to be forgotten. Sometimes they want to remember, but the programs kick in and they forget."

IB: "There are people who do remember. People who don't get affected by the drugs or technology used to make them forget."

G: "Yes, there are many people who do not forget their abductions or physical communication with ETs or Ultra-dimensional beings... But these individuals will often keep their experiences to themselves for various reasons."

IB: "How many species would you estimate are presently abducting or having direct contact with humans?"

G: "Hundreds. There are those races that have a very long and deep connection with the human species, there are not many of those. There are hundreds of species that have had passing or superficial contact with humans."

IB: "We touched on the subject of DNA and ET interest in the human species and mixing their own DNA with humans before. We briefly talked about the Annunaki. There is a belief, and something that I have seen also, that talks about the Annunaki having created humans to be work drones on Earth. Basically slaves. But my own people, the Mapuche, talk about us having been created by Celestial Beings to protect the Earth, humans and all of Earth's creatures. Are Native Americans from a different ET species?"

G: "Not many people realize it, but some of the distinctions in human races on Earth are because they have DNA from different ET species."

IB: "I read a book called 'ENCOUNTERS WITH STAR PEOPLE: Untold Stories of American Indians' by Ardy Sixkiller Clarke. Some of the stories she told are of how Eskimo Native American tribes tell that they were brought here by Sky People from a planet that is cold and icy, and that is why they populated such cold and icy environments, and even flourish there where others would perish within hours if left to attempt to survive there. She also shares the stories of many people who do fully recall their abductions, and how some of them are warned that if they tell about their abductions, they will be eliminated or their families will suffer. Some instead choose not to say anything for fear of being called crazy or losing their jobs or social standing. Some believe that society is not ready to know about these things. The interviews did share that there were many reasons why a person who remembers does not tell of their experience."

G: "Yes, that is accurate."

IB: "The Mapuche, from the Southern parts of Chile and Argentina, have a powerful and unwavering energy of protecting nature and the environment. My conversations with a Machi told of her role, and the Mapuche role, of being exactly that. The caretakers, and guardians of Earth, nature, animals and humans. The origin story of the Mapuche says that Celestial Beings brought them to Earth to be caretakers. She also spoke of how not all people are human. I was visiting her with another person at the time, she took one look at him and told me he was not human. She was surprised that I was with him and told me she had heard that there were plenty of humans in other countries, so could not understand why I would be with a non-human. I didn't understand that at the time, but things became much clearer and different after that. Are there really people walking around the Earth that are not human?"

G: "In that particular situation, we need to look at the cultural and semantic context of her words. For her, a human person will have certain characteristics, such as being open and connected for example. Not afraid to be seen or perceived. The person's core energy would also indicate whether they met or did not meet the Mapuche's definition of being human. There could be other cultural and perception markers for who is human or not human to a Mapuche."

IB: "Yes, on our way to the reservation, our guide who was the husband of one of the tribe members, told us that we would probably be ignored by the Mapuche and that they would behave as though we were not in the room. He told us that they cannot be sure if a stranger is human or not, so the person needs to either be introduced by someone they know as being human, or recognized by the Machi as human. I thought that was very strange at the time."

G: "They have a long history of people and beings pretending to be human, or we might change that word to humane, and find out later on that they were not who they pretended to be. The Native American cultural nature to believe and trust in the word of others has been used relentlessly to destroy them."

IB: "Oh man… that has been one of my vulnerabilities. I will trust people at face value. And honestly think and believe that they are being honest, honorable and truthful at all times. Even when they blatantly lie to me, and I know they are telling a lie, I accept their words as being for a good reason. This has created untold suffering and pain in my life. But for some reason, I can't learn that some people are dishonest and without honor. Being street-smart does not come easily to me."

G: "Yes, it is a vulnerability for someone like you in an environment where people are disconnected from each other and the environment.

The Native People of the planet have taken great losses and pain due to it. But I would say, don't cover up that core essence. In the near future, the human collective will re-learn to unite and will again have no secrets from each other. When that day comes, this particular trait will be a great strength."

IB: "There are lots of things that Native people see as strengths that have been used to destroy them. Trusting the word and honor of another is one of them. Also, the strength of *coup* is another. The way in which a warrior would physically touch his enemy but then choose not to kill him, that being much braver and more powerful experience than simply killing him. Or the dances and rituals that some tribes will use to express their strength and power to the enemy in a display, and in that way their enemy could gage their strength, potentially avoiding armed conflicts altogether. All those are seen as weaknesses by modern society, and modern warfare simply kills and destroys from a distance. Any and all compassion or restraint from the opposing forces will be used as an opportunity to kill or destroy them.

I have experienced this in my own life. Not in a war-like situation, but at a personal relationship level and even at a business level. Actually, now that I think of it, I did experience it at a war level. In the Chilean right-wing coup of 1973, the biggest vulnerability in my family and those people in government was the trust they put in their armed forces to never turn their guns against the population."

G: "Yes, it is difficult to stay in a trusting and honorable place when the people around you repeatedly use it to your detriment. But like I said, persevere, it is not a weakness. It is important that you do not lose that, and that the people around the planet who carry that trust, don't lose it. Yes, like you say, become more street-smart, but don't lose your default sense of trust."

IB: "I can sense from you that this is very important. Can you tell me if that's right and why it is so important?"

G: "That sense and default of trusting in another's words is one of the doors that allow the reconnection of the human species to each other and to the environment to be even possible."

IB: "Oh man… so it's super important but makes us vulnerable. Great."

G: "Trust in yourself too. You can make correct decisions regardless of what other people say or promise if you stay connected, and do daily connection exercises, to your higher self, your core self, the human collective and Gaia. It might sound like mumbo jumbo or naïveté, but if you take your time, take notice of red flags, and spend time at your highest vibrational expression, those people who lie to you won't be able to hold on to you or have any significant effect on you. It is only when you fall into fear, or are disconnected, that you are vulnerable to those lies and dishonesty."

IB: "Are you saying that the Native People became vulnerable to lies and dishonesty because they were in fear or were already disconnected? I mean, I knew that they had disconnected way before the Europeans made contact, but did not know that was why they were vulnerable to lies."

G: "Lies happen even among Native people. But yes, although their disconnect was lesser than the people who have conquered the planet, whom you might call Europeans, they were still disconnected enough to become vulnerable."

IB: "I am aware that the Native people of Europe were systematically eliminated hundreds of years before Europeans travelled the world looking for more land to conquer. I am also aware that Europeans were not the only races that destroyed Native people or that functioned from a disconnected core self. There is broad history in Africa, Asia and Australasia that show of conquerors destroying and totally eliminating tribes and people who would not submit to their rule. There was, and still is, a policy to destroy or make illegal the practices and the support of shamans, healers and other connected individuals around the world. My question is, how can you allow this to happen? If your role is to protect and guide people to their highest potential and experience, why have you allowed this destruction of connected and intuitive individuals to happen?"

G: "Ultimately, we do not rule what your species chooses to experience. Ultimately, if a person, whether they are a wise shaman or knowledge keeper, a reborn guide for humanity, or any person who is here to raise the vibrational frequency of the planet, falls into despair, pain, fear or dogma, we cannot protect him or her."

I could not help but feel self-conscious when he said those words. I myself had fallen into despair, pain and fear so many times in my life and had nearly been killed or destroyed completely by others. I held my now empty cup of tea and moved it back and forth between my hands. To say I felt stupid and naive was to put it mildly. Gabriel reached forward and held my hands still.

G: "In days gone by, you would have had the communal and cultural support to hone in on your abilities and skills. Including your capacity to see clearly, perceive clearly and make educated decisions. You, and countless others around the planet, have come in into the most dark and oppressive period in human history and have had no education, support or training. It is not your shortfall that you were vulnerable. It is your strength that you can overcome your lack of support and nurturing by seeing the bigger picture. It is your strength that you have chosen to wake up and express your highest self regardless of the attacks, fear and destruction around you. And I am not just saying this to you, but to every person who is reading or hearing these words."

A tear escaped my eye.

G: "Can you feel it? Can you sense that there are millions of individuals out there who are ready to step into their true selves without fear, or regardless of fear? Can you feel that what you are teaching and doing, including meeting me and writing a book about it, is going to help shift them out of fear and despair and allow them to follow their hearts?"

IB: "Yes. I can feel it. My trust in humanity has been unwavering. When I fell deeply into despair or fear, my trust did wane, I have to admit that. But as soon as I was able to reconnect to my core self, it was full on again. No matter what happened in my life, or how others behaved toward me, that trust in humanity always returned. Of course, nowadays it is much easier, when I look at the data from our website, millions of unique visitors using the tools there, and thousands of interactions from people stepping into their power and making themselves visible, processing their fear. Receiving all their support and willingness to take on the work. It is much easier for me to have full trust in humanity than ever before."

Gabriel smiled as he squeezed my hands and released them. I smiled back. My heart felt full of love and happy as my reconnection to our human collective was reestablished once more.

G: "It is a moment to moment thing. Although there are people who stay connected and fully aware one hundred percent of the time, most people have to make an effort to reconnect because daily living, and those people around them who are asleep or have open doors to negativity, will wear them down."

IB: "I hear you."

Chapter Nine

We spent the rest of our visit that day talking about the weather and some personal issues I was going through. It was mostly chit chat, and a loving way to wind down the high emotions I had felt during our interview.

Larry had been asking if he would ever meet Gabriel in the flesh, and I was not quite sure why they hadn't yet met. Gabriel suggested that perhaps it was simply a matter of time, or it could be that our bodies have a strong sense of other physical bodies that are not human but look like they are human, and choose not to see them. Sometimes Larry would indeed walk in during our visits but all he would perceive was that the room was exceptionally cold. When we are opening ultra-dimensional portals, the perceived temperature will be ten or more degrees lower than the rest of the house or room, or location. The temperature change can be felt out in nature too. When Larry and I went to Montserrat in Spain in 2014, we were walking on a mountain trail when we suddenly both felt a drastic temperature change. The trail was identical on either side of the temperature bubble. As I tapped into the frequency there, I sensed the Lemurian vibrational signature. It was not long after that, that we were able to enter their dimension. But that's a story for another book.

The next time I met Gabriel, and the last, was during one of our hikes here in the Makah Reservation. We have many trails at the reservation, some are easy and accessible to most hikers, but others are extremely hard and challenging. It was on one of these second ones that Larry and I were hiking when Gabriel made an appearance. It was two weeks after our last visit, and although there had been lots of times when I could have called Gabriel, I resisted doing so. I felt very strongly that our interview project was coming to an end, and was delaying saying goodbye.

Larry and Missy, one of our dogs, decided to climb down a steep rock face to the beach below. I was already tired from the long hike, so decided to lie down on the moss and, as I put it at the time, express physically and energetically fully and without filters. It was a very safe location to do that, I didn't know if my body would change shape and didn't want to freak anyone out. Yes, that has happened in the past.

As I lay there and relaxed into full expression, I heard footsteps through the forest. I sat up and I listened carefully. There are lots of wild animals in the forest in the reservation, and generally speaking it is not always a good idea to hike or take a nap alone in the wilderness. As I listened, I could tell the noise was being made by two people. I could now hear them chatting too. A man and a woman. I recognized the man's voice instantly, it was Gabriel.

I stood up and watched through the brush as they approached. They were both wearing full hiking gear, including gloves and backpacks. I giggled as I watched them navigate the uneven, and mostly hidden, terrain. Gabriel looked up and waved at me. The woman next to him smiled broadly and waved also. I knew her, but from where? I smiled and waved back.

As they got closer, I noticed that there were nearly unperceivable sparkles of light all over the woman's black curly short hair and dark skinned face. Some sparkles were also visible on her clothes. Suddenly I remembered. She was one of the angels who had held my hand and flown with me in the angel dimension! I reached into my pocket and turned on the recorder in my phone.

Interview Nine

It took them a few minutes to reach the smooth, mossy area I had chosen as my resting place. They pushed the last branches away from them and flopped own on the moss, taking off their backpacks and breathing heavily.

IB: "Drink some water, it helps to stay hydrated. You might want to take off your jackets too, it can get hot under all that heavy gear."

They thanked me for the advice and after a while, they were both rested and comfortable. I looked over at the woman.

IB: "I am so happy to see you again. I can't describe how surprised I am that you are here."

Yarelie: "And me too. We were never properly introduced, my name is Yarelie."

IB: "Urielle?"

Yarelie laughed.

Y: "No, that would be one of our brothers. Yes, our names sound very similar to human ears."

She then spelled her name out for me, Y A R E L I E. Pronounced *yaur ah lee*. I looked up the meaning of the name on the internet, and what it means is "she shines". It made total sense to me.

I was still amazed at the fact that she was here in our world, but also at the sparkles of light all over her.

Y: "You can see those? I tried to mask them."

She frowned at Gabriel, as though referencing a conversation they had already had.

G: "You can hardly see them at all. Like I said, I'm sure most people won't see them."

The next couple of minutes were spent with them going back and forth about what the other had said or not said. It make me laugh. They looked at me and started laughing at the silliness of the argument.

IB: "Well, to be honest I can't say in full certainty that I can see the sparklies with my physical eyes. If I look very closely, they vanish. What are they?"

Y: "My usual physical expression is mostly what you might call sparkles of light. I don't spend much time in the human reality construct, and this is my first time expressing as a human body. It is very challenging."

IB: "I am so honored that you have chosen to come visit me Yarelie. May I ask why you are here? Apart from wanting to be around my awesomeness of course."

My joke went unnoticed.

G: "She insisted."

Y: "When I heard that your meetings with my brothers were coming to an end, I didn't want to miss the opportunity to meet you in your own surroundings. Your species has always fascinated me, and although my work is elsewhere, I wanted to see and experience what it was like to meet with you in yours. Plus I have so many questions. It is not often that we get the opportunity to have face to face conversations with other species."

IB: "You don't? That really surprises me. There are so many species in the multiverse, and there are so many people on this planet who profess to having direct contact with your species."

Y: "I have probably not expressed myself properly. Yes, we do have a lot of contact with humans and other species, but usually it is of a service or guidance type interaction. Having full explorations and conversations on the nature of our origin and function is very unusual."

IB: "I have to admit that it is highly unusual for me too."

I looked over at Gabriel.

IB: "I'm going to miss you so much."

G: "We don't have to stop meeting. Once this book project is over, there is no reason why we can't continue our conversations, or just hang out together."

IB: "Intellectually I know this. But I know me also, and I know that once I start concentrating on a new novel I may forget to call you, Gabriel. And before I know it, it might be years before our next meeting."

G: "We can remedy that."

IB: "How?"

G: "Give me permission to initiate our meetings. That way I can come visit you anytime without having to be invited."

I thought about this very deeply. The implications of giving an angel full access to me whenever he wanted triggered my human privacy programs.

G: "I promise I won't turn up while you are having a shower again."

I frowned. I had been thinking about our conversations in the shower when he made an appearance right there in the bathroom. I had explained to him that we humans don't generally feel comfortable with our friends being in the bathroom while we are using it. But, how would he know not to come in while I was having a shower if he didn't take a look in the first place?

IB: "How will you know I'm not in the shower or on the toilet for that matter, if you haven't already looked?"

G: "Oh, I can't check? Well, that does create a problem. What if I connect with you telepathically first, and ask you for permission to visit? That will ensure I don't have to look first."

IB: "Yes, that works for me."

I still didn't feel comfortable telling an angel I was sitting on the toilet, or having a shower, when he connected, but it was preferable than him looking in, or simply appearing in the bathroom.

IB: "You have my permission to initiate visits and contact with me whenever you want, as long as you telepathically contact me first before you arrive where I am."

Y: "It is difficult for us to comprehend your need for privacy. Or the reasons behind what social situations are private and which ones are not. But, like I said, we haven't had an opportunity to have these types of interactions many times before, so we are still learning. We are quick learners, and once one of us learns something, our entire species learns it. Are there any other situations during which we should not visit you?

I blushed profusely.

IB: "Well, yes. When we are going to the toilet is one. Do not appear in the bathroom while we are going to the toilet. And also, and this can happen in all sorts of locations, when two people are making love. Do not butt in while two people are making love."

G: "What if one of you is in danger? And we need to interfere or give guidance because a major decision has been taken or is being considered in that moment?"

I held my head in both hands. It was so easy to forget that the adult man and woman in front of me were not actually human and did not have the same programs and social conditioning that we have.

IB: "OK, if a person who is using the bathroom, or making love somewhere, is in immediate danger, you may pop in and help them."

G: "What if they are not in immediate danger, but they are thinking or planning something that will put them in danger at some future time, but are thinking or planning it while they are using the bathroom or making love?"

I stared at Gabriel unsure of how to respond.

IB: "Hmm. Well… You can visit them afterward and tell them."

G: "We don't always have access to people. And if that moment in time is missed, we may never have the opportunity to guide or warn them again."

IB: "OK, if that's the case, if it's a life altering thought, then yes, you can pop in and talk to them while they are in the bathroom or making love."

G: "What about if it's a moment of enlightenment, where they need advice and guidance that could accelerate their awakening? You would be surprised how many people have those while going to the toilet, are in the tub, having a shower or making love."

IB: "OK, OK. Yes, if it is a moment of enlightenment, you may also pop in at any time, whether they are having a shower, are in the tub, going to the toilet or making love."

Yarelie whispered something in Gabriel's ear.

G: "Does making love include situations where the person is sexually stimulating themselves with no other person in the room?"

I wished the earth would open up and swallow me.

IB: "Yes. It does. If it is a situation where there is one or more consenting adults, involved in sexual activity and there is an immediate or future danger to themselves or others or loss of opportunity for growth involved, then yes, you can drop in unannounced."

They both expressed they understood the difference between an appropriate time to come into the room, and an inappropriate time to come into the room, or location.

Y: "Can I ask a question?"

I nodded.

Y: "You are able to morph into different physical expressions. I saw this while you were with us in our collective awareness."

I sighed deeply very relieved that the conversation about privacy was over.

Y: "And even now I can perceive some non-human characteristics in your body. Like the shadow, or remnants of a different physicality. I am fully aware that this is a characteristic in some human races. The capacity to shape shift, or morph into different shapes. Yet, it is not a usual thing even among the species in the universe. We can do it, and do it all the time, and there are species who do it. Although some human races are capable of doing it, not many people in those races know how to. How did you learn to tap into that skill? And do you do it often?"

I remembered that before they appeared, I had made the intent to fully express in my true form. But when I realized that some people were approaching, I returned to my human form. That Yarelie would see the remnants of my true physical expression as not human gave me pause for thought. But then I realized why she perceived it that way.

IB: "Well, I find that each person who sees or knows me, perceives or sees me in a different shape. For example, one person sees me as very dark skinned, with small eyes and thin lips, and a hooked nose. Another person sees me as pale, with big eyes, red hair and thick lips. Other people look at me and see a Native American woman. Others see me as a Spaniard, or European. Many people in Ireland would see me with red hair and pale freckled skin. A lot of people see me and think I look like a relative, such as their mother, sister, daughter or grandmother. Or even one of their close friends. When they send me photos of the relative or friend, I can see that there is no actual physical likeness. The local Sasquatch even saw me as a baby sasquatch, and warned me well away from the edge of a dangerous cliff, and no amount of explaining that I was able to watch out for myself was enough to convince them to reduce their concern."

Y: "You are saying that the way you look is not so much dependent on your physical expression, but the visual data interpretation of the person who is looking at you?"

IB: "Yes, that's an excellent way to put it. I'm a bit of a wildcard, a person who looks like or fits into the role of what the other person most needs to see or be near at the time. I personally don't feel very solid to myself, or find it easy to keep one uniform physical form for any length of time. So, what we should be asking in this particular situation, what do you see, and what do the non-human characteristics you see in me mean to you personally."

Y: "Hah! OK. Well, that does surprise me. I can feel my awareness expanding and exploring the possibilities of this situation."

Yarelie looked deep in thought for quite some time.

Y: "OK, I perceived remnants of a species I have known and worked for in the past. It is a very evolved species, they are of a physical nature not unlike that of humans. We might call them humanoid. They have a reptilian DNA base. Their spiritual base is highly evolved and was secondary only to their drive to explore the multiverse."

IB: "What sort of thoughts or emotions come up for you when you think about them?"

Y: "I admired them deeply. I had more than one incarnation in their species, born and lived as one of them. I have great respect for them. But also, I miss them. I long to be with them again, spend time and work with them. It's so weird, I have not thought of them for millions of your linear Earth years."

IB: "Well, one might be able to interpret that as perhaps your inner self telling you that you need to find them again. Maybe it's time to reestablish that relationship and connection in your life."

Yarelie's eyes swelled with tears. She rubbed her eyes in surprise and gasped for air as she repressed crying out loud. Gabriel hugged her but she was still highly distressed. I wanted to reach out and touch her hands but felt it might make things worse, so stayed back. Gabriel told her to breathe deeply and release the air quickly and powerfully. I remembered how he had learned to use that method on one of our first meetings to calm the emotions he was feeling.

IB: "Angels have a much larger emotional body than we humans do, and when you express in human form, your human emotional body can get overwhelmed. It will pass."

Gabriel breathed in deeply and released the air quickly. Yarelie followed suit. A few minutes later she was smiling. She reached into her backpack and pulled out some tissues, cleaned her face and breathed deeply. She looked at Gabriel.

Y: "My respect for your work in human form, in this planet is now beyond words. I never realized how challenging it is to express in human form. My respect expands to all souls who choose to embody as humans. It is indeed very challenging, and difficult."

IB: "Would you like to explore the reptilian race you have such a deep connection with? Or would you like to talk about something else?"

Y: "Your features, the ones that are barely perceivable, are like those of one of my sisters in the last incarnation I had with them. My sister and I became very close, we were inseparable. We decided to study the same topics and launch in the same work path as Explorers. This race has a very long life span compared to yours, of about ten thousand of your linear Earth years. We married into the same family, male cousins of what you might call a spiritual or shamanic lineage, who were also explorers. The four of us travelled and explored the universe for thousands of years. My mate and I did not have children, by choice, but my sister did and her children were brought up by all of us. It was a happy and long life. After my sister died in an ultra-dimensional accident, I was not able to overcome the heartbreak and sadness I felt. I died of a broken heart soon after. I swore I would never again return to that species, and would never get attached to one of their people again. Or any non-angel for that matter. Once we disconnect, it's often not possible for us to find a being who belongs to another species. I knew that trying to find my sister was a futile exercise. Even if I had found her again, she would be in a different expression and would not remember who I was. My own race's role within their reality is that of spiritual guide. Had I found her, and had she perceived me, she would have related to me not as her sister, but as her spiritual guide. That was not a role or relationship I felt capable of efficiently having with her."

I felt the waves of pain and loss she was feeling. Another human trait, empathy. Not always the best trait to have stimulated while in the company of angels. But my emotional body was now much stronger and able to handle angelic emotions to a limited but useful degree.

I tapped into her personal timeline, looking at that particular lifetime. It was indeed a joyful and very expansive life. I tapped into her sister, felt her vibrational signature, and found her in present time. I knew that this feat would be impossible without the other being's permission, especially as I had never had any type of interaction with the sister. Or in this case, him. Yarelie's sister was now incarnated as a male. A powerful and influential religious leader of his people. He'd had several incarnations both as men and women after the life he shared with Yarelie, and in all of them there was a gap, a longing to reconnect with his sister. Although it was not a conscious drive, it had, through lifetime after lifetime, led him to have a deep and strong connection with their Source, making him an exceptionally gifted spiritual leader. I wondered if it was appropriate to share this data with Yarelie.

My focus returned to the two angels sitting in front of me, and saw that somehow, they were seeing what I was seeing. Their eyes open wide and slightly out of focus.

IB: "Oops."

Y: "It's OK."

G: "Sorry, I forgot to say, since you shared your consciousness with us and temporarily became part of our collective, when we are in the same energy field your and our consciousness can become one. When we saw you looking at something important, we instantly connected with you. There was no thought or resistance, or any type of information that would tell us it was not allowed. And it is something we do automatically among ourselves. It only occurred to us that maybe that was not your intent when you wondered whether to share the experience with Yarelie."

IB: "Actually, it makes things much easier for me. Now I don't have to make a judgment call about it. Not only that, it's hard to express multi lives and their essence in words. Now you got the full load of information yourself and can make educated choices regarding contact with your sister. Who is now your brother I suppose."

I said the last bit directly to Yarelie.

Y: "I have to sit with this and explore it. I need time to look at her lives, at her now, and overcome my own sense of loss before I can make a decision of whether to contact her again or not. And it's not just her. It's the entire species. I became too close, or too attached, to be an efficient guide to them."

G: "It's one of those things, more common than you would think. Sometimes we get so involved in a species, or individuals within the species, that we can no longer do our jobs properly. That's usually a strong indication to move on to another species or project. As most of us stay with one species or project for millions of years, you can imagine how difficult this choice is for us to make. The choice to step away I mean."

IB: "Talking of millions of years. There is a huge disparity of data, both historical and cultural, with regard the age of the human race. Exactly how long have we existed? And is Earth our planet of origin?"

G: "That's a question that not many people have asked. In order to respond, we would need to make a clear definition of what constitutes a human being."

They both looked at me, as though waiting for me to give them the definition of what constitutes a human being. I thought about this for a while. My mind was racing at the possibilities of why we needed such a definition. The definition could potentially limit the answer, exclude information that we might want to hear. Up until that moment, for me a human being was a symbiotic relationship between a soul who could have come from any dimension or planet, and a physical body recognizable as human, made up of Earth materials. Yet, from the information they had given me, and the data gathered from Native cultural memories, this was not so accurate. It appears that many human races have been brought here by extra-terrestrials, or ultra-dimensional beings. Some, like the Maya, believe they are the extraterrestrials who arrived on Earth, then lost their memory of the technology needed to travel the stars.

Yet there are no human races on the planet that cannot intermix, who cannot have children with each other. I wanted to think of a definition that included all the races on Earth, yet did not exclude the possibility of these races having come from elsewhere. The word *definition* meant to set bounds on something. Bounds would limit the answer, but it didn't have to be permanent. I needed to think of a definition that would include all the data that was relevant for this particular discussion, but also limit the answer to workable and understandable information.

IB: "For this question, the definition of a human being, is a being who has a soul which is incarnated in a physical body that we would call a person in appearance and has the DNA and building elements common to all human races on Earth, but not limited to having originated or presently existing either on Earth or in the timeline or dimension we are presently in."

As I said these words, I could tell I had already limited the response in a drastic way. I could sense that being human could come in many other shapes and elemental constructs. But, for now, I wanted to get answers only relevant to the human races we have on Earth. Exploring other expressions of human existence would have to wait.

Y: "That is a definition we can work with. As to your first question, how long has the human race existed? I can say that it has always existed both in linear time and outside of linear time. Within this broad definition of what a human being is, Earth is not the planet of origin for human beings."

I waited, expecting a more thorough answer.

IB: "When you say that humans have always existed, both in linear time and outside of linear time, do you mean to say that we didn't have a moment or place of origin? That we were not in fact created by evolution or by a different species?"

G: "From what we have seen, human beings have been limited by other species, but not created by them. There are human beings on other planets that have not been limited by external species. The general consensus is that human beings are a way to express and experience the physical universe by multiple soul constructs, both original souls as well as artificial souls, or engineered souls. Therefore humans are highly coveted by different species who have worked tirelessly to manipulate human expressions that will serve their purposes. And yes, as far as we can perceive, humans do not have one point of origin in time or space. One might more accurately actually say that time and space originated within the human experience."

My mind was racing at a thousand miles a second with the possibilities this line of questioning was opening. I wished I had my notebook so I would not lose certain enquiries while exploring others.

IB: "Who came first, the human species or the location they originated from? It's a bit like the chicken or the egg question. I do understand that it is not a question you are able to answer right now. When you say that other species have manipulated human expressions to serve their purposes, what sort of purposes do you mean?"

G: "We have encountered multiple purposes. Some have to do with evolution of their own species, some have to do with the creation of planets that will support their own species. Some will create workers, slaves, caretakers, or rulers of peoples for the sole purpose of the conquering of planets and dimensions for the physical enrichment of their own species. Generally, in these last cases, their own species is unable to physically occupy or exploit said planet or dimension."

IB: "This makes sense if we take into account that we, humans, are the creators of physical, experiential reality. Put enough humans in a barren environment, and they will transform it into a lush and supportive location. It also makes sense why certain beings are investing so much money, time and effort to create fear around the Earth. Billions of humans in a state of fear, creates a very low frequency environment. A low frequency environment is not supportive or nurturing to humans, but it is so to other entities."

Y: "Yes, we have identified the same issue that is present on Earth right now. At a different level, humans throughout space, time and dimension are connected to each other no matter where the soul in each body originated from. There seems to be limits or barriers to how humans, as a broader consciousness, are willing to be used. Barriers that limit the frequency and vibrational signatures in which humans are willing to create environments within. Your birth, and the birth or incarnation of millions of people whom you might call of being of a high frequency, or feel the urge to awaken themselves and others, heal the planet and each other, nurture and support Gaia, all these people are the firewall that automatically comes on when the human race… or we might more accurately say, human technology, is used by a species to create low frequency environments. The planet known as Earth is also conscious. And the humans who were here co-creating a reality with the Earth did decide to experience a low frequency reality, allowing the entrance of beings from low frequency dimensions and universes to coexist here. This is not something that is normal or usual for the human technology to accept. Yet, it appears that as a species, humans decided they did want to experience it. It does broaden the full spectrum of experience for humans. But, as low frequency universes and entities are by default conquerors, they could not coexist, but instead wanted to use the human technology to expand their low frequency real estate. Human technology allowed them to move only so far, but now it is putting a stop to the whole thing. Thus the birth of you and millions of others who are here to raise the frequency of the planet."

G: "I would also like to add that the conversation we had a while back, about us all travelling somewhere, how all the species who interconnect are all in some way or another obsessed with evolution or expansion seem to be obsessed with travelling to the very same place is also related here. The low frequency universe and beings are also in that same journey, so it's not that much of a stretch to see why the human race would agree to have a co-created and interconnected experience with them."

IB: "I have always felt that human beings ultimately chose to have this low frequency experience, and that now they were done with it. But I didn't realize it was a multiverse, multi-dimensional and multi-planetary decision. I thought it was just Earth. Why didn't you tell me this before?"

G: "We are limited in our conversations with different beings to their cultural and reality perceptions and constructs. In other words, until you see a larger or broader picture, we cannot communicate about that larger or broader picture."

IB: "That poses a lot of limitations on what we can explore together. I mean, if you cannot originate information that is outside of my realm of experience or belief system, how can I move past it into a broader state of awareness and perception?"

Y: "It might seem like it's a decision we have taken, but the opposite is true. We often, and regularly do express broader realities to humans, and other species, but the result is that the information gets filtered and interpreted within the constructs of culture and reality the being has. It is not us putting up the barriers and limits, but the being we are communicating with only being able to perceive and understand within the limitations of their own reality."

IB: "The misinterpretation, or hijacking of information by our own cultural, social or religious programs or our own ego. Yes, Gabriel and I discussed this already."

Knowing that this was a common occurrence was the reason I would record my conversations with the angels and transcribe them as they were, and limited my own interpretation of what they said to a minimum. Still, even that can be hijacked, so I always suggest that a person reading or listening to my stuff be their own judge and authority to its accuracy.

IB: "Some of the origin stories of Native people's on Earth talk about either being from other planets, or having been placed here on Earth in a certain geographical location by extraterrestrials, or Star People. You have already stated that humans do not originate from Earth or anywhere that we know of. So my question is, what defines a Native or Indigenous person as opposed to a non-Native person?"

G: "We work very closely with all people of Earth, no matter what their race or cultural, religious or social background is. I am saying this to illustrate that our exposure to humans is not race related or limited. Saying that, we have observed that the souls that incarnate into human bodies here on Earth are not limited by race. Many souls, most souls in fact, have incarnated in all the human Earth races through different linear time incarnations. Although some souls do resonate and prefer to incarnate in one race above all others. The definition of what constitutes a Native person as opposed to a non-Native person is related to the physical body. Basically where the body was born in a geographical area, as well as a cultural and social viewpoint. Yes, some species did come to Earth and settled here, becoming Native to specific geographical areas. And yes, some Native people were re-housed, we might say, by different species from different planets into very specific geographical areas. Areas where these particular humans would not only flourish, but maintain the reality of that location. So, for example, a human race that flourishes in a dry, hot climate, would keep that geographical area perpetually dry and hot. All races on Earth, whether Native or not, have been altered at a DNA level to have certain predispositions, drives, and are able to flourish in different geographical locations."

IB: "I can see and understand that definition, and analysis, of what makes a person Native. But you haven't defined what makes a person non-Native in nature."

G: "We might say that a Native person stays, or has a predisposition, to stay within a limited and defined geographical area and within one cultural and social construct that supports them and that they support and create through time. Even when the Native race is nomadic, they will stay within certain geographical areas, and often do not marry outside of their own race or culture. They will also often not have any desire or drive to impose their own DNA or culture onto other races. A non-Native person not only does not have these predispositions, but in fact will go out of their way to expand their own geographical area, will impose their own culture and belief systems onto other races, even if these cultural and belief systems do not support the other race, and will generally have an animating force of conquering space and time that is not limited to Earth. Like the Native races, what we define as non-

Native were also placed here on Earth either by themselves or by other species, yet are not limited to stay within their culture or geographical location."

IB: "Well, within that definition of what is a non-Native person, we could say that even the Inca Empire was non-Native then. They conquered huge areas within South America. Yet, today we qualify Incas as being Native Americans."

G: "The Inca was one man. The ruler, king, god of the Inca Empire. A title that was passed from father to son. The Incas were conquerors, that is true. And brutal when it came to any other Native tribe that did not agree to be ruled by them. Yet, they were very accommodating and flexible when it came to maintaining the other tribe's original culture and geographical area if they did agree to pay tribute to the Inca. Also, the other tribe was ordered to release certain religious, social and cultural beliefs that the Incas regarded as offensive, and basically submit to peace within the Inca Empire. The tribe, in turn, would be economically and structurally supported by the Inca Empire. In other words, although the conquering family, the Inca, we might correctly say was not Native in nature or predisposition, the tribes within the Inca Empire were."

IB: "We often think, or define, a non-Native person to be white or of European descent. Yet, when I lived in England, Ireland and Spain, I met many people there who would most certainly qualify as being Native. They were connected to the land, had an inner drive to stay there, had a culture specific to their geographical area and were distinct in appearance to people from other places in those countries. Some still speak local languages. So, although white, they are still Native."

G: "Yes, it is a misconception to think that all Native people have dark skins or are not from Europe."

IB: "I suppose a more modern definition might include the concept of living within a tribe. I mean, the modern concept of a tribe and not the original meaning which basically means 'three' and referred to the three divisions of the early people of Rome, who had distinct cultural and blood relations from each other. Although blood and cultural direct relationships can still be said to be what constitutes a tribe today."

Y: "I think that this is one of those situations where putting too limiting of a definition onto a people is counterproductive. What you consider as a Native person has been defined by your laws throughout the planet. And at an instinctual level, most people on Earth will be able to recognize a Native person as opposed to a non-Native person and vice versa."

IB: "No kidding. Half of my DNA is Native American, a quarter is Spanish, and the rest is divided between Irish, Gypsy, Jewish, Greek and Italian. Legally, I was classified as a child as a white Caucasian. Yet most people, Native and non-Native, who meet me immediately assume I am Native American. Except a handful of Native Americans, who had a very strong reaction against me, classifying me as a white oppressive conquistador. Going back to our roles within the planet. It feels to me that the world is now divided between those people who want to maintain a clean and supportive environment, and those who prefer to exploit nature and Earth and the nature of humans as reality creators, for their own benefit. There are many Native people who are actively involved in the protection of their environment. But also, many non-Native people who are also involved and highly active in that goal. When I was talking to the Machi, Mapuche leader, in the South of Chile, she told me that many humans were being born in Europe and around the world. Again, I don't have a clear definition of what she meant to be human, but from the context of her definition, I think she meant Native people were being born around the world into other races. Would that explain why so many people of all races are being driven to protect nature and our species?"

G: "I know it can get confusing. And this is one of those times when your own limits of reality is placing a belief, or label, onto what is happening here and now. My suggestion would be to stop thinking locally, and start thinking at a multi-planetary and dimensional level."

Y: "Think less on the human races on Earth and which ones are overtaking the others, or which ones are protecting the environment, and more on the concept that the human technology at a multiverse level has decided that the infusion of low frequency, which we might call the drive to conquer and destroy all others, is now being removed from Earth."

I thought about this for a while, and could clearly see how my own limitations, both cultural and social, were limiting my understanding of what Yarelie and Gabriel were expressing.

IB: "I have a huge sense of identification and resonance with all species and races, both planetary and non-planetary. Whenever I look at a group of people or species whether they are divided or driven by DNA or culture, I feel love for them. I understand their drives without judgment. But at a daily life level, I get utterly frustrated at the limitations of human and other species actions, reasons, and drives. I cannot understand why they don't see the wider picture. Obviously there are thousands of people and species who do get it. Who do see the wider picture. But it feels like the majority of human beings, and multiverse beings do not."

Y: "Again, I would suggest that you, and everyone who is awakening, embodying the new paradigm as you have expressed, stay focused on the job at hand. To stay embodying and expressing high frequency vibrations. To support the reconnection of the human species with each other and with the larger collective. To consciously and purposely use your power to this end. Not to get sucked into drama or low frequency engagements, and when they do, when you do, to quickly move out of those low frequencies."

IB: "It's so easy to lose focus. I would also add that if the person is inspired to take physical action as a protector or guardian of Earth, humanity, or society, they do so from a place of high frequency energy, not as a reaction to fear, anger or frustration. To process all those low frequency emotions and beliefs first, like the belief of righteousness, and then act from a level of awake and conscious choice."

I heard Missy barking and knew that Larry was on his way back. Yarelie and Gabriel smiled and starting picking up their gear. My heart felt heavy at the knowledge that this would be our last interview. But the thought that Gabriel now had full access to visit whenever he wanted brought me comfort.

IB: "It was so wonderful to see you again Yarelie. Please feel free to visit along with Gabriel whenever you like."

Suddenly there was a super strong gush of wind, and we all instinctively crouched down to the ground. A bright and fiery light landed next to us, in the form of Michael.

We all shouted out his name at once, and Gabriel and I ran over to hug him. Yarelie watched us full of curiosity. I guess she wasn't familiar with human hugs as a form of greeting yet.

G: "Brother, it is so good to see you again outside of the whale entity."

IB: "Michael, you are a sight for sore eyes. I was really worried that you might get stuck being a whale, that you would forget you are an Angel."

Michael who towered over both of us, spread his wings and embraced us both with them. He then rubbed the top of our heads with his knuckles, like one would do a child.

M: "Yarelie, what a wonderful surprise. Gabriel, Inelia, enough with the cuddles. Ok, one more minute."

IB: "What are you doing here?"

M: "I didn't want to miss the opportunity to say goodbye. Your human lifespans are so incredibly short, if I blink I might find you dead for thousands of years of linear time, and I may not see you incarnated again. I just wanted to see you here one more time, say thank you and also let you know that I am here if you ever need me or want to hang out."

My eyes filled with tears.

IB: "Wow. That means so much to me. Thank you Michael."

I could swear he vibrated whale like, almost like the ocean was inside of him. He eventually pushed Gabriel and I away and walked to Yarelie, giving her a hug too, which she reciprocated.

I could sense that they would walk away any moment, and I could not help my tears from welling up.

IB: "I'm going to miss you so much guys. Please know my door is always open to each of you. Only you three though, unless someone else requests to visit, then we can take that on a case to case basis…"

I laughed at my own sense of being cautious and limiting in who I allowed into my life. Even when it involved angels.

IB: "Yarelie, if you would like to reconnect with your sister, now brother, let me know. I have some ideas. Gabriel, you are my angel, I love you so much. Michael, although we didn't start out so good, please know that I love you too, and totally get you. I don't think you get me yet, but maybe you do. I'd like to be your friend and would love to get to know you better."

The next few moments were spent saying goodbye and promising to meet again. Then Michael flew up and away, and the two hikers walked back into the forest.

A few minutes later Larry arrived with Missy, "did you have a good nap?" He asked. "Not exactly." I responded as I wiped the tears from my face.

Postscript

Since that last meeting, I've had visits from all three angels, plus a few more who visited with them. Gabriel suggested I should write about our visits in a second book, but I'm busy writing a novel about the Annunaki at the moment. I've kept notes, and if I get the time I will certainly share the further adventures I've had with these amazing beings.

My last words here would be for you, who is reading this, to carefully examine your own constructs of what an Angel is, move away from a standpoint that they are in any way superior to us. Perhaps redefine them as simply one of millions of extraterrestrial or ultra-dimensional beings out there.

Although I did not express it, it felt to me that Angels are also expressions of a more expanded definition of what a human being is. They certainly have many of the same drives that we do. And although they are not creators of reality, they most certainly protect and work with humans and other creator species in our realities and chosen paths. They express many of the characteristics we assign as humane.

And last but not least, don't forget that this book is legally classified as a novel.

Printed in Great Britain
by Amazon